BASIC SEMINOLE PATCHWORK

Cheryl Greider Bradkin

D1097631

Leone Publications
2628 Bayshore Drive, Mt. View, California, U.S.A. 94043

Copyright © 1990 by Cheryl Greider Bradkin

Editor: Joan Pederson

Production: Terri Wanke

Printed in Singapore

ISBN No. 0-942786-50-5
10 9 8 7 6 5 4 3

Table of Contents

My first introduction to Seminole patchwork was a skirt my mother bought in Florida in 1941, but it was not until 1977 that I began to research the technique. Finding no books available for sewing details, I used my mother's skirt and sketches of designs from Seminole Indian clothing in National Geographic photographs and worked out construction techniques, first with drawings and then with fabric. The next year I began teaching the technique at The Quilting Bee in Los Altos, California. The owner of the shop, Diana Leone, encouraged me to write my first book, which was self-published with 16 designs in black and white. That book was expanded and published in 1980 by Marti and Dick Michell with over 60 designs and color. In a satisfying closing of the circle, this newest Seminole patchwork book is published by Diana Leone, now the owner of Leone Publications.

Another progression in this publishing history is technological. My first book was hand written, with the earliest printing made on a copy machine. The second book was produced with traditional printing techniques for typesetting and color separations. This third book was composed on my Macintosh IIcx computer (except for the photographs), using the software programs Word™, PageMaker™ and Illustrator™. My rise to a computer author and designer was made possible by the unfailing good humor of my family and friends. I am grateful to Bill and Lisa for their love and patience, to Morris and Roslyn Bradkin for their moral support, and to Gene and Norma Greider for their joie de vivre. Special thanks goes to Ken Rhee for first putting his Macintosh in front of me and saying "just try it."

Since the 1980 book, some things have changed! Husband Bill still bicycles off to teach at the college each day, but our Lisa, who was six years old in the 1980 book photographs, is now a Design major at UCLA. We live in the same house in northern California, but a studio addition has given me creative space and a 16 foot wall for fabric storage. My dirt gardening interests have waned while my Seminole fabric gardens are growing—but that's another book....

Create and enjoy!

Cheryl Greider Bradkin

Seminole Indian creations, circa 1940

The origins of Seminole patchwork go back to the early 1900s, when Seminole Indian women in the Florida Everglades developed the technique. Using hand-cranked sewing machines and cotton broadcloth in dazzling colors, the Seminoles created their striking patchwork garments. The technique is simple but yields patchwork that gives the illusion of complexity.

The basic technique is to sew strips of fabric together, cut them into pieces, and then sew them back together in different positions. From this simple yet almost magical concept, thousands of design variations are possible.

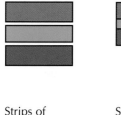 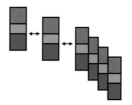

Strips of fabric

Strips sewn into a strip set

Pieces cut from the strip set, offset, and sewn together into a patchwork band

The patchwork band finished off with edging strips

The Seminole patchwork technique

Many Seminole patchwork designs imagined on a larger scale bring to mind contemporary quick quiltmaking techniques. One can only speculate on whether machine strip-piecing and quick-piecing methods had their roots in the Seminole technique developed nearly a century ago.

This book is designed for use by anyone interested in patchwork, from beginners to experienced piecers. The first three chapters establish a firm foundation by introducing recommended tools and their uses, defining the terminology, and explaining the most successful methods for each step in the construction. Beginners will find the frequent illustrations helpful, so the methods can easily be understood. Those experienced at Seminole patchwork will probably pick up a new tip or technique in Chapter 3 that will make their work more accurate, faster, or easier.

Detailed instructions for wonderful projects, as well as suggestions for using Seminole patchwork in your own creations, are contained in Chapter 4.

Chapter 5 presents recipes for 56 Seminole patchwork designs, making it a valuable reference section.

The techniques for mirror image and graphed designs in Chapter 6 are a bit challenging and are included for the patchwork artists wanting to expand on the creative possibilities of Seminole patchwork.

Whether your style is traditional or contemporary, there is a place for the Seminole technique in your patchwork.

Measurements throughout this book are offered in inches or centimeters. The measurements are not interchangeable, so choose one system to use.

1. Tools and Materials

Tools

Sewing Machine

Seminole patchwork has always been a machine technique, which is part of its appeal. It is sewn using an easy, fast method that is absolutely authentic! It requires only a straight stitch machine with dependable thread tension and smooth fabric feed. A sewing machine that zigzags is helpful for finishing some projects, such as applying Seminole bands to towels, but is not required.

The width of the sewing machine presser foot is important for Seminole construction. The seam allowance used throughout this book is 1/4" (0.6cm), so the ideal presser foot measures 1/4" from the needle to each outer edge of the foot. Even with an ideal presser foot, it is easier on the eyes to keep fabric edges along a 2" (5cm) tape line placed on the throat plate of the machine, instead of staring at the edge of the presser foot. An accurate way to place the tape is to sew through a piece of 1/4" graph paper, with the right edge of the paper cut along one line and the needle piercing the next line to the left. Place the tape along the edge of the paper.

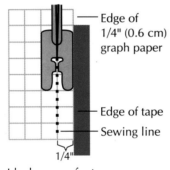

Edge of 1/4" (0.6 cm) graph paper

Edge of tape

Sewing line

1/4"

Ideal presser foot

Narrow presser foot

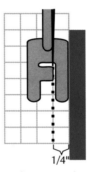

1/4"

Wide presser foot with adjustable needle

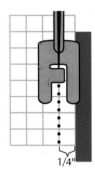

1/4"

Wide presser foot with non-adjustable needle

Using graph paper to place tape for 1/4" (0.6cm) seam allowances

Some machines have an adjustable needle position. Refer to your manual to set the needle position 1/4" (0.6cm) from the edge of the foot for an accurate 1/4" seam.

Masking tape is commonly used to make the fabric guide but 1/4" wide shiny plastic charting tape sold in graphics supply stores is great. It has a nice clean edge and comes in colors.

When sewing designs containing 3/4" (1.8cm) wide strips, you will probably want to set up the machine for using the 3/4" Strip Technique described in Chapter 3.

Serger

A serger is an optional tool that trims and overcasts the seam allowances as the seams are sewn. A serger can be used to finish off the patchwork seam allowances on projects that are not lined. Use of a serger for sewing the small pieces together is not recommended because matching the pieces is difficult and the stitches are hard to remove.

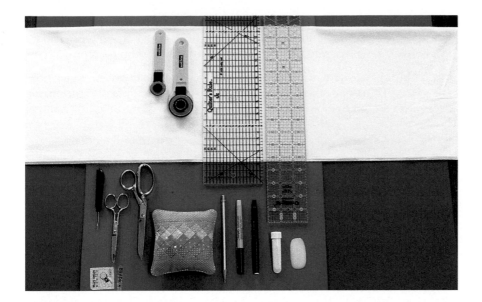

Tools used for construction of Seminole patchwork

Of all the new products that became available to fabric artists in the 1980s, the rotary cutter is the most revolutionary for Seminole patchwork. This round blade mounted on a handle cuts through single or multiple layers of fabric. It is used along the edge of a cutting guide for straight cuts. Looking back on my early work, with the fabric marked with pencil and then cut with scissors, I can see that the rotary cutter not only saves time but also adds accuracy to every step.

My favorite rotary cutter is the large size Olfa™ because it cuts well against plastic rulers used as cutting guides and has a blade safety guard that clicks securely into position.

Take care when using a rotary cutter because it has a sharp blade. Cut at a table of a comfortable height, with your body squarely in front of the work. Grip the rotary cutter by the handle with fingers away from the blade. Hold the cutting guide in place with your hand flat on the ruler. Place your little finger on the mat and the rest of your fingers and thumb on the cutting guide clear of the cutting edge. With the blade against the edge of the cutting guide and the cutting motion away from the body, cut through the fabric with firm, even pressure. *Always* snap the blade guard into place before setting the tool down.

A rotary cutter blade will last a long time if it is used to cut only cotton fabric. Eventually the blade will have to be replaced. Take the cutter apart carefully and pay attention to the order and placement of each piece. When assembling the spring, it should sit like a bowl. The nut is then screwed into it.

Rotary cutting is done on a special plastic mat to protect both the cutting surface and the blade. Mats are available in many sizes, in different types of plastic, and with or without grid markings. Grid markings can be helpful but are not necessary for Seminole patchwork.

A small 6" x 18" (15cm x 45cm) mat is a good size to take to workshops, and a large 24" x 36" (60cm x 90cm) mat is a useful size at home or in the studio. The largest 3' x 6' (90cm x 180cm) mat makes a seamless worktable cover. Garment pieces can be cut out on the larger mats, using weights to hold down the pattern pieces and cutting freehand.

The softest mat is slick on one side and pebbled on the cutting side and can be pinned into if needed. A slightly harder mat, also pebbled on the cutting side, is designed as a worktable cover. The Olfa™ mat is of medium hardness

Rotary Cutter

The rotary cutter used in this book

Cutting Mat

with a smooth, matte texture on both sides, making it reversible. All of these mats must be stored flat and kept away from heat. The hardest type of mat is thermoplastic with a very slick surface; it can be rolled up for storage.

If it is a problem to store mats flat, they may be hung on the wall. Make holes 1/2" (1.2cm) from one edge with a grommet die and a hammer or cut triangular holes with the point of a mat knife, and hang the mats on headless nails.

Scissors

If you do not have a rotary cutter, a pair of sharp 8" shears will work fine if they can easily cut through several layers of fabric. Small 5" scissors or thread clippers are handy for cutting threads.

Iron

A good steam iron and careful pressing techniques can make Seminole patchwork behave well. Keep the soleplate clean and do not use a clip-on soleplate cover, which interferes with the temperature control and the steam. If only a dry iron is available, have a misting bottle nearby to dampen the patchwork before pressing.

Rulers

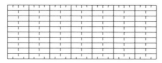

The ruler used in this book

Rulers used in Seminole patchwork must be transparent and have grid lines, which are lines in both directions. In addition to measuring, rulers are used as cutting guides with rotary cutters, and the grid lines are used to align right angle cuts. Some rulers also have marked lines for 45° and 60° angle cuts. Of the many rulers in my studio, my favorites are the 6-1/2" x 24" Quilter's Rule™ and the smaller Quilter's Rule Jr.™ by Betty Gall, with textured grid lines to help keep the ruler from slipping.

Markers

One of the advantages of using a rotary cutter and gridded transparent ruler is that most marking is eliminated. To make measurement marks for angle-cut pieces, use a dark felt tip pen or soft, light markers such as a chalk pencil, silver pencil, or the last sliver of a bar of soap. To mark offset lines, which should not show through the fabric, use a soft sharp pencil, soap chip, or chalk.

Pins

Seminole patchwork goes quickly if you learn to sew without pins, but there are a few designs that require their use. The 1-3/4" (4cm) ball-headed pins are easy to control, and the extra length allows the fabric to lie flat.

Seam Ripper

In addition to its intended use, the seam ripper is great for easing fabric pieces and seams underneath the presser foot.

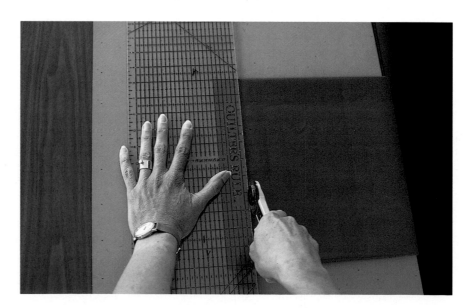

Use of rotary cutter in a comfortable and safe position

Cotton prints and solids

Fabrics

The best fabric for Seminole patchwork is 100% cotton broadcloth. For projects that will require a lot of washing, such as towel bands and children's clothing, cotton-polyester blend fabrics will retain their colors longer. These fabric blends need a little more attention during sewing because they are slightly slippery and the seams tend to appear rippled even after pressing.

The adventurous piecer who wants to use unusual combinations of fabrics should try to keep them all about the same weight. One heavyweight fabric combined with lighter fabrics will distort the lighter weight fabrics. A very thin fabric can be made firm by ironing a lightweight fusible interfacing onto the back. Heavyweight fabrics such as denim work best in larger scale patchwork designs, with strips and pieces that are at least 1/2" (1.2cm) wide when finished.

Prewash fabrics to avoid any shrinkage or dye run later. Fabrics for washable projects should be treated to the same soap, water temperature, and drying temperature that they will receive later. Ready-made shirts and towels onto which patchwork will be applied should also be prewashed and dried.

Thread

Use any good quality sewing thread in a color that blends with most of the fabrics used in the patchwork. As long as the stitch tension is correct, it is not necessary to match the thread color to the fabrics.

If there is a definite progression of colors in a project, it is worthwhile to change the thread color to blend with each section. If one color in a project is white or a very light pastel, consider using that color thread throughout, so any loose thread ends on the back of the patchwork will not show through the fabrics in the finished project.

2. Terms Used in Seminole Patchwork

Strip

A strip is cut with the lengthwise or crosswise grain of the fabric.

Strip Set

Strips are sewn together at their longest edges to make a strip set. A single design may be made up of several strip sets. In this book, the length of a strip set is 42" (105cm), the width of most fabrics.

Piece

A piece is cut from a strip set.

Straight-Cut Piece

A straight-cut piece is cut at a right angle to the seam lines of the strip set.

Angle-Cut Piece

An angle-cut piece is cut at any angle other than a right angle to the seam lines of the strip set.

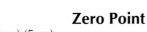

Zero Point

The zero point is the left end of a strip set, where measurements begin for one method of marking angle-cut pieces. Zero points are shown in the design diagrams if they are needed.

(7.5cm) (5cm) (5cm)
3"   2"   2"

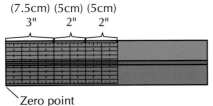

Zero point

Nonidentical Piece

Some designs are composed of nonidentical pieces either cut from different strip sets and sewn together, or cut from the same strip set and sewn with every other piece upside down.

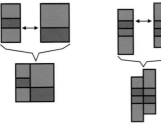

Pieces from different strip sets

Pieces from the same strip set

Nonidentical pieces are sewn together to create a design unit, shown enclosed in a green box. Completed design units may be sewn together in any order.

Design Unit

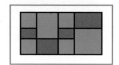

Two points, which may be seam lines, marked lines, or other distinct points on the pieces, are match points used for alignment of the pieces in the offset position. The example shows seam lines as match points.

Match Point

Pieces are offset before being sewn together. The offset is an alignment different from the original position in the strip set. The offset for each design is shown by an arrow between the match points in the design diagrams. The first example shows the offset at a seam line and a marked line, and the second example shows the offset at a seam line and a distinct corner point.

Offset

Chain sewing is a timesaving technique for sewing pairs of pieces together. The seams of pairs of pieces are sewn without stopping the stitching between the pairs.

Chain Sewing

Pieces are sewn together in offset positions to form a patchwork band.

Patchwork Band

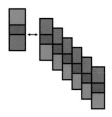

Edging strips are used to finish off the long jagged edges of the patchwork band. Several edging strips may be used to complement the design and color of the band and create the desired width.

Edging Strip

Patchwork band ready for edging strip

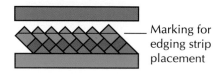

Marking for edging strip placement

---

3. Seminole Patchwork Construction

Use of Color

Color to Set Mood

Color is too personal a subject to make rules about, but these considerations may help a project succeed. Seminole patchwork can look cheerful in crayon colors, dreamy in muted pastels, moody in Amish colors, sophisticated in black and white, festive in bright, clear colors, or earthy in neutral tones. In other words, there is a Seminole patchwork look for every project, from the obsessively sedate to the irrepressibly zany.

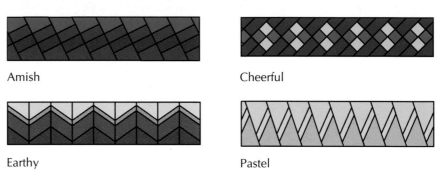

Amish

Cheerful

Earthy

Pastel

Color sets the mood for the patchwork

Success in color choices for the desired effect depends on contrast. Strong contrast in color, such as green and orange, or in value, such as ivory and black, will make a striking and highly visible patchwork design. Less contrast in color, such as blue and green, or in value, such as mauve and tan, will create softer looking designs that emerge only with close viewing.

Prints to Create Interest

Tiny prints on fabrics that look like lively solids from a distance are wonderful used together or mixed with solids. In selecting tiny prints and solids, it is important to view combinations from 5' and 10' (1.5m and 3m) to see how the effect changes with distance.

Combining several medium- and large-sized prints can interfere visually with patchwork seam lines and obscure the patchwork design. A single larger print can successfully combine with solid fabrics. The larger prints should be considered from several viewing distances before being used.

Preparation of the Fabric for Cutting

Quilters buy some pieces of fabric in 1/4-yard (0.25m) cuts and other pieces in 3-yard (3m) lengths. When combining fabrics with such varying yardages, it is most convenient to cut strips for Seminole patchwork with the crosswise grain so that all the strips are about 42" (105cm) long or equal to the width of the fabrics.

Begin by pressing the fabric. Half-yard (0.5m) cuts are most convenient, so to save time if a piece of fabric is over 1/2 yard (0.5m) long, leave the length intact but prepare only about 18" (0.5m) at one end for cutting. Fold the fabric in half, holding the selvages together in the air so that the fabric hangs into a fold. Adjust the alignment of the selvages until there are no pulls in the fabric along the fold.

Lay the fabric on the ironing board and press in the first fold. Working on the ironing board, fold the selvages so that they lie parallel to *but are not covering* the first fold. This creates the second fold, which is also pressed. The grid lines on the ruler cutting guide are aligned with the folds as the strips are cut.

If a fabric is printed with an obvious design that you want to follow, do not fold the fabric. Cut only single layers at a time, using the transparent ruler to determine the best placement for the strip. Include 1/4" (0.6cm) seam allowances on each side of the printed design.

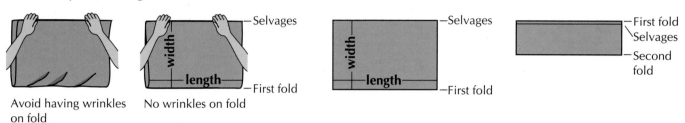

Folding the fabric with the selvages even   Folding the fabric to create the second fold

Construction of Strip Sets

Move the folded fabric to the cutting mat. Place a gridded ruler on the fabric with one short grid line on the second (double) fold and another short grid line parallel to the first (single) fold. Trim one raw end (see illustration a). It is important that the fabric, ruler, and rotary cutter are always used in a comfortable and safe position. To accomplish this during the change from trimming the end to cutting the strips, turn the fabric 180°, turn the entire cutting mat with the fabric on it 180°, or walk around to the opposite side of the cutting table (see illustration b).

Locate the long grid line on the ruler cutting guide that corresponds to the cutting width of the strip. Place this line on the previous cut, check that the short grid lines are parallel to both folds, and cut the strip (see illustration c).

If the strips are cut at right angles to both the folds, each strip will be perfectly straight. If the cut through a fold is at any angle other than a right angle, the strip will have "Vs" at the fold lines. The gridded ruler is important because when the short grid lines of the ruler are parallel to both folds in the fabric, any cut made along the long edge of the ruler is at right angles to the folds.

Cut the Strips with a Rotary Cutter

After cutting strips, fold the remaining fabric so that the freshly cut edge is protected during storage. The next time you want to cut a strip of the fabric, the protected edge will be ready to use.

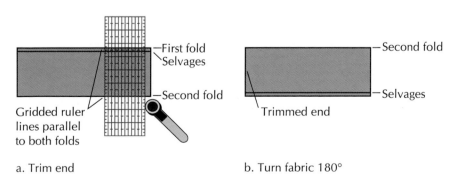

a. Trim end   b. Turn fabric 180°   c. Position ruler and cut strip

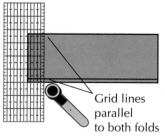

Cutting strips using the rotary cutter

Cut the Strips with Scissors

In this book the cutting tool of choice is the rotary cutter, but scissors will work. Fold the fabric and position the gridded ruler in the same way as described for the rotary cutter. Mark the cutting line with a soft, sharp marker. Place pins down the center of the marked strip to hold the fabric layers together. Cut along the marked line with scissors. If several strips are being cut from the same fabric, mark all the cutting lines before placing the pins.

Sew the Strip Set

Whenever a strip will have a 1/4" (0.6cm) finished width, use the 3/4" Strip Technique (page 18).

All of the sewing in this book uses 1/4" (0.6cm) seam allowances. If you have not already done so, it is worthwhile to take time now to mark the sewing machine throat plate so that it is easy to sew consistent seam allowances. Use 12 to 16 stitches per inch (2.5cm), small enough not to pull loose at cut edges but not so tiny that they would be difficult to remove.

Make any necessary machine adjustments before beginning a project. When thread tension and presser foot pressure are perfect, sewing is a pleasure.

Working with a short section of the strips at a time, it is easy to sew without pins. Align two strips for about 6" (15cm), and sew them together for about 5" (12cm). Stop with the needle down in the fabric, so that the strips will not move. Align the next 6" (15cm), sew that length, and so on.

Resist the tendency to pull on the top strip as you align the edges for sewing. If the top strip is stretched while sewing, a curve will develop in the strip set. Also, always add the newest strip underneath the strips that have already been sewn together.

Press the Strip Set

Some sewing machine beds have edges that catch on the seam allowances of butted seams and cause the fabric to bunch up. A piece of transparent tape will make ramps out of the edges and eliminate this problem.

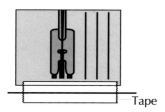

Tape

A piece of transparent tape will smooth the way for the seam allowances to pass over

Press all the seam allowances in one direction, toward the bottom of the strip set, or as indicated by the pink pressing arrows in the design diagram. The seam allowances of the pieces in most designs will point toward you during sewing and will feed smoothly between the feed dog and the presser foot. Some designs have butted seam allowances in which the seam allowances on nonidentical pieces are pressed in opposing directions. Seam allowances, when butted, aid in the alignment of the seam.

Press the strip set one time after all the strips have been sewn together rather than pressing each seam as it is sewn. Press from the face side so that the point of the iron can open and flatten the fabrics along the seam lines, eliminating any tucks along the seam lines. While pressing, use the fingers of your free hand underneath the strip set to smooth the seam allowances in the proper direction. Check the wrong side of the strip set to be sure the seam allowances are smooth and flat. The pressed strip set should appear straight and even. If it does not, relax the fabrics with spray from a misting bottle and press more carefully to unbend curves and even out the widths of the strips.

No marking is required when using a rotary cutter and gridded ruler to cut straight-cut pieces. Each piece is cut at right angles to the seam lines of the strip set. Each cut becomes the starting point for the next cut.

First trim off one raw end of the strip set with the short grid lines of the ruler parallel to the seam lines of the strip set (see illustration a). Turn the strip set 180° (illustration b). On the ruler cutting guide, locate the long grid line that corresponds to the cutting width of the piece. Place this line on the trimmed end, keeping the short grid lines parallel to the seam lines of the strip set. Cut the piece (see illustration c). Then use this new cut as the starting point for measuring the next piece.

Cut Straight-Cut Pieces

Align the short grid lines with the seam lines of the strip set rather than with the outside edges of the strip set.

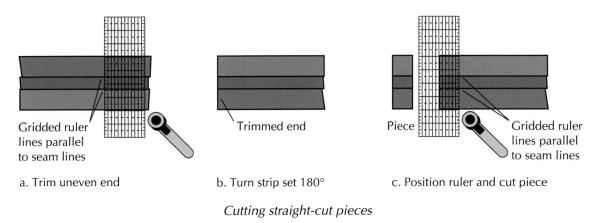

Gridded ruler lines parallel to seam lines

Trimmed end

Piece

Gridded ruler lines parallel to seam lines

a. Trim uneven end   b. Turn strip set 180°   c. Position ruler and cut piece

Cutting straight-cut pieces

If scissors are used, position the gridded ruler in the same way but mark the cutting lines with a soft, sharp marker. Cut on the lines with scissors.

There are two approaches to marking and cutting angle-cut pieces, depending on the type of transparent gridded ruler being used. For the first, Method One, you may use any ruler; the second, Method Two, requires a transparent ruler with marked lines for 45° and 60° angles.

You may notice in the design diagrams that the measurement marks when using any ruler (Method One) and the cutting width when using a ruler marked with angles (Method Two) are different dimensions. This is because of the geometry of angle-cut pieces; the dimensions are correct.

Method One – Using Any Ruler: If you are using a ruler that does not have angle lines, you will need to make measurement marks along both long edges of the strip set and then connect the marks and cut the pieces. Making the measurement marks takes very little time and assures a precise result. Each design diagram shows what the measurements should be.

The measurement marks are made on the very edges of the strip set with a felt tip pen or other soft marker. A hard marker would ravel the edge of the fabric. Correct ruler positions are shown in the illustration on the following page. Rather than moving the ruler for each mark, it is better to position the ruler and mark as many measurements as possible along its length before repositioning it. See the illustration on the next page.

Mark and Cut Angle-Cut Pieces

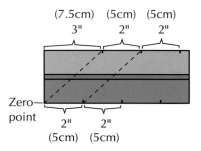

(7.5cm) (5cm) (5cm)
3"   2"   2"

Zero—
point   2"   2"
(5cm)   (5cm)

Typical design diagram for making measurement marks for Method One

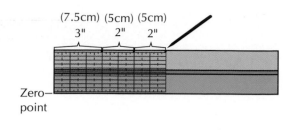
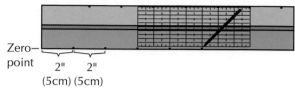

(7.5cm) (5cm) (5cm)
3"   2"   2"

Zero—
point

a. Mark top edge of strip set

Zero—
point   2"   2"
       (5cm) (5cm)

b. Mark bottom edge of strip set

Making the measurement marks for Method One

The first cut always connects the zero point on the bottom of the strip set with the first measurement mark on the top.

Position the ruler cutting guide to connect the zero point on the bottom of the strip set with the first measurement mark on the top of the strip set. Cut from the bottom zero point to the first top measurement mark along the edge of the ruler cutting guide. This cut is the correct angle for all the pieces for that design. It cannot be emphasized too much that the first cut is from the zero point on the bottom of the strip set to the first measurement mark on the top.

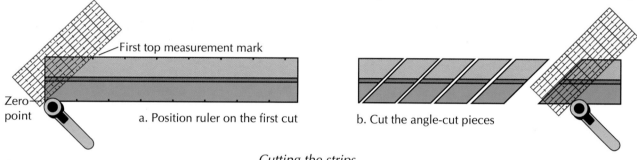

First top measurement mark

Zero
point   a. Position ruler on the first cut

b. Cut the angle-cut pieces

Cutting the strips

Always connect the measurement marks at the points where they touch the outermost edges of the strip set.

Cut the rest of the pieces by connecting the next set of bottom and top measurement marks and cutting along the guide.

If scissors are used, draw lines connecting the measurement marks as shown on the previous page and cut along the lines

Method Two – Using a Ruler with Marked Angle Lines: Many transparent quilting rulers have lines marked for 45° and 60° angles. These lines can be used to continuously check the angle of cuts, so the previous cut can be used as the starting point for measuring the next piece. Each design diagram for an angle-cut design contains the angle and the cutting width for the pieces. As shown in the illustration, the appropriate angle line on the ruler is placed parallel to the seam lines of the strip set, and the first cut is made along the long edge of the ruler cutting guide. To cut each piece, the long line on the ruler corresponding to the cutting width of the piece is placed on the previous cut. The angle line on the ruler is kept parallel to the seam lines of the strip set as each piece is cut.

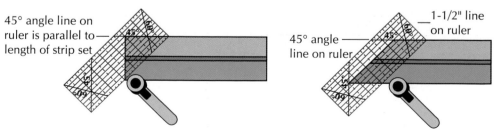

45° angle line on ruler is parallel to length of strip set

a. First cut at 45° angle

1-1/2" line on ruler

45° angle line on ruler

b. Piece cut at 45° angle and 1-1/2" wide

Using a ruler with angle markings for Method Two

Construction of the Patchwork Band

As the pieces are cut, pile them up and place them near the sewing machine in the orientation shown in the design diagram. Take two pieces, align them as the arrows in the design diagram indicate, place face sides together, check the alignment again, and sew with a 1/4" (0.6cm) seam allowance.

To make the alignment of pieces more accurate, check the alignment at the point where the new seam line will be, 1/4" (0.6cm) inside the edges of the pieces. It is usually adequate to pinch the pieces tightly together as they are sewn. If the pieces slip, use a single pin to hold them. Some angle-cut designs require the use of a pin for a successful match, as indicated in the design diagrams. Pins are rarely necessary for designs with butted seam allowances.

Chain sewing is used to save time and thread as the pieces are sewn into a patchwork band. When you sew the first pair of pieces together, sew to the very bottom edge of the pieces, but do not break the thread or lift the presser foot. Align another pair of pieces and begin to sew at the very top edge of the pieces. Continue in this manner and soon all the pairs of pieces will be sewn into a chain. When there are no more single pieces to pair up, reach around behind the machine and clip off some pairs of pieces. Open out two pairs, align them, and sew them together. After all the pairs of pairs are sewn together, sew pairs of fours together. Continue until all the pieces are sewn together into a single band of patchwork.

Sew the Pieces Together

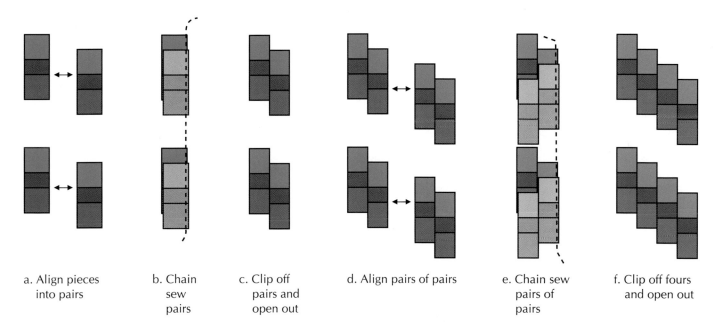

| a. Align pieces into pairs | b. Chain sew pairs | c. Clip off pairs and open out | d. Align pairs of pairs | e. Chain sew pairs of pairs | f. Clip off fours and open out |

Chain sewing pieces for designs with identical pieces

To chain sew designs with nonidentical pieces, the order in which the pieces are sewn must be organized to sew complete design units. The organization for Design 10 is shown below.

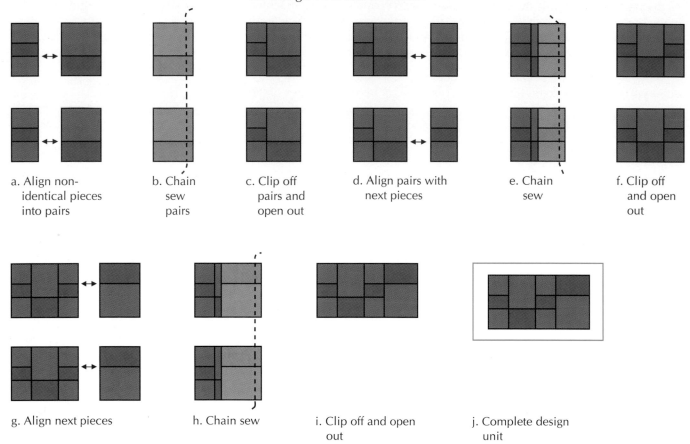

a. Align non-identical pieces into pairs

b. Chain sew pairs

c. Clip off pairs and open out

d. Align pairs with next pieces

e. Chain sew

f. Clip off and open out

g. Align next pieces

h. Chain sew

i. Clip off and open out

j. Complete design unit

Organized chain sewing for designs with nonidentical pieces

In the design diagrams, a green box encloses a complete design unit. The completed units may be sewn to each other in any order.

Designs with 3/4" (1.8cm) wide pieces will be sewn together using the 3/4" Strip Technique (page 18). If each design unit is sewn together from the *right* side to the left side of the design diagram, the 3/4" (1.8cm) wide pieces will always be in the correct position for using the technique.

Press the Patchwork Band

Most designs should be pressed with all the seam allowances going in one direction on the back. Press the band from the face side so that the point of the iron can remove tucks and flatten the fabric along the seam lines. Use the fingers of the free hand underneath the band to smooth the seam allowances all in one direction. Press with the straight grain of the fabrics as much as possible, rather than with the length of the band of patchwork.

There are a few designs with angle-cut pieces that look best if the seam allowances are pressed flat in whatever position they choose to lie. The design diagrams will indicate when this pressing technique should be used.

The completed band should appear straight and even. If it does not, use steam and more careful pressing to straighten it out.

Attachment of the Edging Strips

The construction of most Seminole patchwork designs creates jagged long edges. Covering the jagged edges of the band is an exciting step in the construction, as the beauty of the patchwork design emerges.

Decisions about edging strips depend on the size of the area to be covered and on whether the effect should be visually simple with a few wide edging strips, or more complex with many edging strips. The number, widths, and colors of the edging strips are part of the creative process, so this is a time to experiment. Lay out the patchwork bands and try different combinations of edging strips on them. Usually there are odd bits of fabric left over from the patchwork to play with, so it is not necessary to cut into the yardage intended for edging strips until exact widths have been determined.

One color formula that is almost always successful is to use the outermost colors of the patchwork band in reversed positions for the edging strips. Then, inner colors from the patchwork can be used for additional edging strips.

Experiment with edging strips that show the finished width. When cutting the actual edging strips later, remember to include the seam allowances.

The ideal placement for the first edging strips is with the sewing line spaced at least 1/8" (0.3cm) from the outer design points of the patchwork band. If the sewing line is closer, minor irregularities along the line of outer design points will be very noticeable. Many designs in this book allow a 1/4" (0.6cm) space between the outer design points and the sewing lines of the edging strips, and some have more space.

The sewing lines for the edging strips are designed to be 1/4" (0.6cm) inside the lines of the innermost raw edges of the patchwork band, which are shown in the design diagrams.

With the patchwork band face side up, find the line of the innermost raw edges and place the long edge of the gridded ruler along this line.

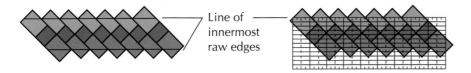

Positioning the edge of the ruler on the innermost raw edges for placement of edging strip

At the same time, align one of the grid lines on the ruler with the outer design points of the patchwork to assure that the edging strip will be sewn on at an even distance from the outer design points of the patchwork.

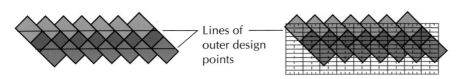

Aligning a grid line on the outer design points of the patchwork for placement of edging strip

Design Edging Strips

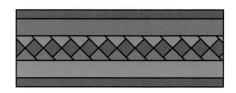

One color formula for edging strips

Mark Edging Strip Placement

You may notice that the outer design points of the two end pieces will not align with the rest of the design points. This is because the end pieces are wider than the rest of the pieces (they still have a seam allowance unsewn). Disregard the end pieces when aligning the ruler with the outer design points.

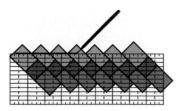

Marking the top of the band for edging strip

Sew Edging Strips onto a Patchwork Band

When a 1/4" (0.6cm) finished size edging strip is sewn, use the 3/4" Strip Technique described in the following section.

With the ruler in this position, draw a line with a soft, sharp marker along the top edge of the ruler, even with the line of the innermost raw edges.

Draw a similar line along the bottom edge of the patchwork band. While positioning the ruler for this bottom line, keep the top line parallel to a grid line on the ruler so that both the lines on the band will be parallel. Then the width of the finished band will be consistent.

Place an edging strip on the patchwork band, face sides together, with one edge on the drawn line. Use care not to stretch either layer and sew with a 1/4" (0.6cm) seam allowance.

Whenever possible, leave the jagged edges of the band intact until after the edging strip is sewn in place. With the jagged edges cut off, there is a greater chance of stretching the newly cut edge, which is bias on many designs. Also, the pieces could begin to pull apart once the extra stitches created in the chain sewing are cut off.

When both edging strips are sewn on, check the finished appearance. If the patchwork band appears even and straight, trim off the jagged edges of the band even with the seam allowance of the edging strip. Add more edging if desired.

Sewing on edging strip

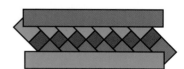

Top and bottom edging strips sewn and pressed

Special Techniques

This section contains construction techniques that apply only to some Seminole patchwork designs or to particular situations. They are included as a kind of fine-tuning section of techniques. As your interest in Seminole patchwork grows, there will be a curiosity about methods that make the sewing as perfect or as efficient as possible. The design diagram will direct you to this section if the design you are sewing will benefit from one of these special techniques.

3/4" Strip Technique

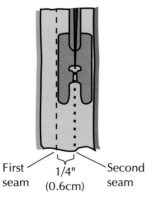

First seam | 1/4" (0.6cm) | Second seam

Sewing the second seam using the 3/4" Strip Technique

The narrowest strips used in this book are 1/4" (0.6cm) *finished* width, 3/4" (1.8cm) *cut* width, and can be sewn using the 3/4" Strip Technique because many presser feet measure 1/4" (0.6cm) from the needle to the *left* edge of the foot.

The 3/4" Strip Technique assures a consistent finished strip width because the first seam line of the narrow strip is used as the guide for the second seam line. Since the two seam lines are parallel, the finished width of the strip is even, and it is the finished width that shows on the face side of the patchwork.

Sew the first edge of a 3/4" (1.8cm) strip to the adjacent strip. Press the seam allowances away from the 3/4" (1.8cm) strip. Position the third strip for sewing with the 3/4" (1.8cm) strip on top. Sew the 3/4" (1.8cm) strip and the third strip together, but *use the first seam line* as the guide for this second seam. The second seam will be 1/4" from the first, resulting in a 1/4" wide sewn strip.

Set up your machine so that the needle is 1/4" (0.6cm) from the *left* edge of the presser foot using one of the following techniques:

- If the left edge of the presser foot is 1/4" (0.6cm) from the needle, keep the left edge of the presser foot along the first seam line.

- If the presser foot is narrow, allow a small space between the left edge of the presser foot and the first seam line.

- If the presser foot is wide and has an adjustable needle position, place the needle 1/4" (0.6cm) from the left edge of the presser foot. Keep the left edge of the presser foot along the first seam line.

- If the presser foot is too wide and the needle position is not adjustable, use it, remembering that the goal is to keep the finished sewn width consistent and even rather than an exact measurement.

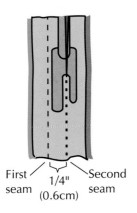

First seam / 1/4" (0.6cm) \ Second seam

Narrow presser foot

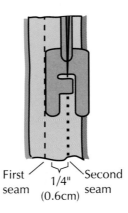

First seam / 1/4" (0.6cm) \ Second seam

Wide presser foot with adjustable needle position

First seam / 1/4" (0.6cm) \ Second seam

Wide presser foot without adjustable needle position produces generous 1/4" width

Different presser feet used with the 3/4" Strip Technique

Most designs have match points at seam lines or other distinct points for aligning the pieces in an offset position for sewing. However, some designs do not have visible match points. The diagrams for such designs will specify an offset distance that must be marked on the strip set before the pieces are cut.

Mark Offset Distance

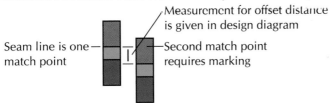

Measurement for offset distance is given in design diagram

Seam line is one match point —

Second match point requires marking

A design requiring a marked offset line for one match point

Sew the strip set and press all seam allowances toward the bottom strip. Turn the strip set to the wrong side, and on the top strip measure the offset distance from the seam line. Mark the offset line with a marker that will not show through the fabric, such as a soft, sharp pencil, a soap chip, or chalk.

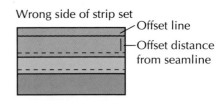

Wrong side of strip set
— Offset line
— Offset distance from seamline

Marking offset line on wrong side of strip set

Cut the pieces. As each two pieces are aligned to be sewn, the top piece will have the marked offset line showing so that it can be aligned with the seam line match point on the underneath piece.

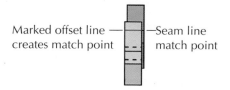

Marked offset line — creates match point   —Seam line match point

Aligning two pieces to sew using marked offset line

Press Bands of Angle-Cut Pieces

As indicated in the design diagrams, some designs with angle-cut pieces distort less during pressing if the seams are not forced in one direction. Simply place the patchwork band face side up on the ironing board, stretch the band slightly, and press the band flat and straight. There will be twists in the seam allowances on the back.

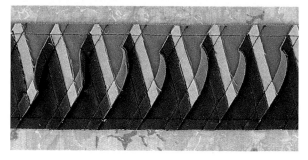

Typical pressed seams for angle-cut pieces, showing face and wrong sides of the band

Straighten the Ends of a Band

Many Seminole patchwork designs produce bands with slanted ends, and the construction of many projects requires straight ends. One could make extra long bands and cut the ends off straight, but that makes odd bits of leftover patchwork. It is better to use the following technique, which makes use of every inch of the patchwork band. This is an optional step because it is not always necessary. For designs sewn with nonidentical pieces, both slanted ends of the band must be complete design units, shown enclosed in a green box in the design diagram. Then the slanted ends may be sewn together without breaking up the continuity of the design.

Cut straight through the patchwork band to create the two new straight ends (illustration a). Sew the slanted ends together, aligning the match points for the design (illustration b). Now the slanted former ends are somewhere in the band of patchwork, the straight cut has made the new ends, and all of the patchwork is usable.

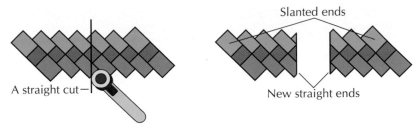

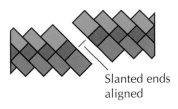

a. Make a straight cut through the band to create two new straight ends

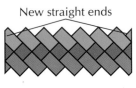

b. Sew the slanted ends together to straighten the ends of the band

Straightening the ends of a band

Sometimes a band of patchwork is wonderful except for one little mistake. Instead of ripping and resewing, make that new straight-end cut right through the mistake and sew the slanted former ends together.

Correct a Mistake in a Band

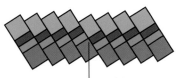 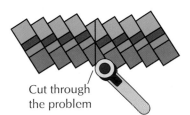

a. Create two new straight ends

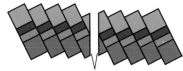 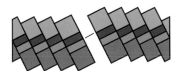

b. Align the slanted ends and sew them together

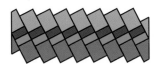

Corrected and straightened band

Removing a mistake and straightening the ends of a band all at once

4. Use of Seminole Patchwork

While it is fun to experiment sewing different designs, real satisfaction comes when the patchwork is made into a unique and useful item. This chapter gives guidelines for projects: decorations on towels, book covers, tote bags, and clothing embellishments.

The bands of patchwork do have a small amount of lengthwise give, but as a general rule the bands should be used to decorate areas that are straight, flat, and stable.

Sometimes the patchwork band is automatically lined when it is topstitched onto an item, such as a towel. In other projects the patchwork is attached to a lining fabric, and the two layers are handled as one in the rest of the construction, for example with tote bag pockets and shirt yokes. There are projects, such as heavy denim skirts or soft rayon dresses, that might become too stiff if the patchwork is sewn to a lining fabric. Instead, use zigzag stitching or a serger to finish off the seam allowances. As each seam or chain of seams is sewn on the regular sewing machine, check the accuracy of the regular stitching and then zigzag or serge the seam allowances. Each seam allowance should be finished off before taking the next construction step, before crossing seams are sewn.

Towels

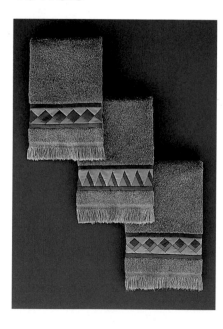

Towels with machine appliqued Seminole bands were some of my earliest projects while learning about Seminole patchwork, and some of those early towels are still in use.

The fabrics of choice for patchwork on towels are cotton-polyester blends. They keep a fresh appearance even after repeated washings. Also, these fabrics yield patchwork that does not require ironing.

Choose only towels with at least one even hemline or fringe line. In a stack of seemingly identical towels at the store, some will have nicely squared off hemlines while others are wobbly. This is especially important to check if towel seconds are being purchased. The Seminole patchwork band is sewn on in a straight line and will draw attention to a crooked hem. Only one end of the towel will be decorated for this project.

Prewash both the fabrics and the towels using the same water and dryer temperatures that they will be exposed to when in use.

Consider the relationship between the width of the patchwork band and the size of the towel. For a set of three fingertip towels, the three patchwork bands should all be the same finished widths. For a bath and hand towel set, the patchwork bands may be the same widths, or a wider band could be used on the larger towel. Washcloths should probably not be decorated, as the band of patchwork might interfere with their use.

Plan the colors of the Seminole patchwork so that both of the edging strips are the same color. Then a single top thread color that matches the edging strips can be used to machine stitch the band onto the towel.

Step 1. Sew the Seminole patchwork band a few inches longer than the towel's dimension so that the design can be centered on the towel.

Step 2. Sew the edging strips onto the band and press under 1/4" (0.6cm) along the long raw edges of both edging strips.

Step 3. The position of the band on the towel depends on the size of the towel and the width of the band. Try out a few different positions to find the most pleasing one. The band should be centered on the towel so that the design concludes at the same place on each end. Turn under the ends of the band where the terry cloth loops meet the flat woven edge of the towel, about 1/4" (0.6cm) from the edge of the towel.

Pin the band to the towel without stretching the patchwork. Place the pins along the edging strips, with the raw edge turned under 1/4" (0.6cm). Verify that the design is centered at the ends of the patchwork band, then trim the ends to turn under 1/2" (1.2cm) and pin the ends of the band to the towel.

Step 4. Match the top thread color to the edging strips and the bobbin thread color to the towel. The band is sewn to the towel with a very narrow zigzag stitch, about 1/16" (1.5mm) in both length and width. Straight stitching can also be used, with the sewing line about 1/16" (1.5mm) from the folded edges. The stitches are eventually hidden by the terrycloth loops of the towel. Begin stitching at one corner and sew completely around the band. Pull all thread ends to the back, tie them off and trim the threads to 1/4" (0.6cm).

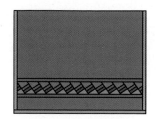

Positioning a band on a towel

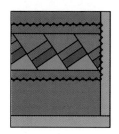

Detail of stitching around one end of the band

Book Covers

Seminole patchwork slipcovers can personalize all those albums and binders that organize our lives, as well as the memo books and checkbooks in our purses. These covers are individually fitted and can easily be removed for washing.

Step 1. Sew Seminole patchwork bands and edging strips together to make an outside cover piece that is at least 1" (2.4cm) larger on all sides than the book when it is opened out flat. Plan the outermost edging strips to be 1" to 2" (2.4cm to 4.8cm) wide, cut from the same fabric as the inside covers.

Step 2. Cut two inside covers 1" (2.4cm) larger on all sides than one cover of the book. Finish the spine edge of each inside cover by turning under twice and topstitching. From the same fabric, cut two spine pieces, 2" (4.8cm) longer than the thickness of the book and about 2" (4.8cm) wide. The purpose of the spine pieces is to finish the top and bottom edges between the inside covers, along the spine of the book.

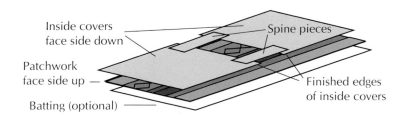

Assembling the layers for a book cover

Step 3. Place the patchwork, face side up, onto the work surface. If the cover is to be padded, cut a piece of thin batting or fleece the same size as the patchwork and place it under the patchwork. Place the inside covers on the

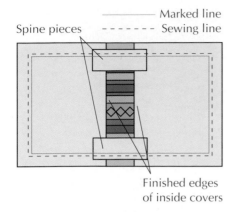

Spine pieces ——————— Marked line
- - - - - - - Sewing line

Finished edges
of inside covers

*Book cover layers ready to sew
together*

patchwork face side down, separated by the thickness (spine) of the book. Place the spine pieces face side down, evenly overlapping the inside covers and about 1/2" (1.2cm) outside the top and bottom edges of the book.

Step 4. Place the opened book onto the cover with the top and bottom edges of the book parallel to the seam lines of the edging strips. Mark around the edges of the book with a temporary marker that will not show through the fabrics (chalk or a soap chip).

Step 5. Pin all the layers together. Along the top and bottom edges, sew about 1/16" (1.5mm) to 1/8" (3mm) outside the marked line, depending on the thickness of the cover of the book. On the side edges, sew a scant 1/4" (0.6cm) outside the marked lines. The extra ease on the side edges is needed so that the slipcovered book will close.

Step 6. Before trimming any seam allowances, leave the slipcover wrong side out and slip it onto the book. Close the book and feel along the edges. There should be a little extra space, which will be filled by the seam allowances after the slipcover is trimmed and turned. When the fit is right, sew around one more time slightly outside the first sewing line, using a very short stitch length. Trim the seam allowances to a scant 1/4" (0.6cm).

Step 7. Turn the slipcover face side out and press it flat with the spine pieces to the inside.

Tote Bags

A tote bag with a Seminole patchwork pocket can be small or large, for use as a gift sack, purse, knitting bag, or overnight carry-all. Since the handle design gives support to the bottom of the bag, the tote bag can also be used to carry heavy workshop supplies.

The body of the bag should be made of a sturdy fabric such as canvas or denim. Most canvas fabrics are treated to repel water and soil and should not be prewashed. The patchwork pocket is lined and has no stress points, so the fabric choice is unlimited. The handles are webbing about 1" (2.4cm) wide, which is available in cotton, polyester, or nylon in many widths and colors.

Step 1. Sew patchwork bands and edging strips together until the piece is 1" (2.4cm) wider and longer than the finished pocket size. The width of the pocket is also the distance between the sides of the handles, so 6" (15cm) to 8" (20cm) is a comfortable size. Cut a piece of lining fabric the same size as the patchwork pocket and sew the right sides together along the top edge, using a 1/4" (0.6cm) seam allowance. Turn face sides out, press the top edge of the pocket, and handle the patchwork and lining as a single layer.

Step 2. Decide on the finished width, height, and thickness of the bag and cut the canvas larger, as shown in the illustration on the next page. To finish off the top edges of the bag, press under 1/4" (0.6cm) and then press under another 1" (2.4cm) and topstitch. Temporarily mark the bottom centerline of the bag.

Step 3. Place the canvas on a flat surface. Place the patchwork pocket in position in the center of the bag front, about two inches down from the top of the bag. Cover the raw bottom edge of the pocket with a length of webbing and topstitch along both long edges of the webbing. The short, raw ends of the webbing will be covered in the next step.

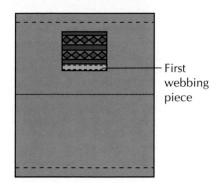

Placing pocket and short webbing piece

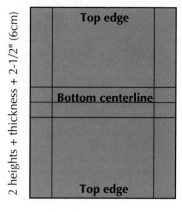

Cutting dimensions for the canvas body

Step 4. Pin the webbing in one continuous length, as shown in the illustration below, beginning and ending with a 1/2" (1.2cm) overlap on the bottom centerline. The webbing covers the raw side edges of the pocket. Allow a comfortable length of webbing for the handles. Beginning and ending at the bottom centerline, topstitch both edges of the webbing on each side of the pocket, stitching a reinforcing X shape at the top edge of the bag.

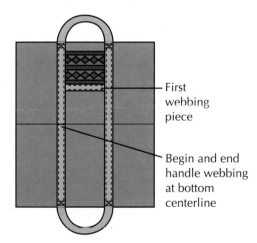

Sewing handle webbing

Step 5. Sew the sides together with a French seam to enclose the raw edges by first sewing the side seams *wrong* sides together with a 1/4" (0.6cm) seam allowance. Then turn the bag inside out. Resew the side seams face sides together with a 3/8" (0.9cm) seam allowance.

Step 6. With the bag inside out, sew the bottom corners of the bag. The seams will be perpendicular to the side seams and the bottom centerline of the bag, and the length of the seams will equal the width of the sides and bottom of the bag.

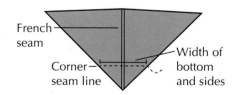

Sewing the bottom corners

Clothing

The American Indian development of Seminole patchwork a hundred years ago was for clothing decoration, and that tradition is carried on today in contemporary garments that are as wild or as subtle as the artist can imagine.

Color and fabric are usually the first inspiration for patchwork clothing. If a garment is sewn in colors that the wearer loves and looks great in, the project is most likely to be a success. In general, highly contrasting color combinations create striking garments that attract attention, while low contrast colors have a rich aspect and can interest the viewer at closer range. Choose fabric types that are appropriate for the amount of wear and laundering that the garment will receive. Children's clothing and other frequently washed items will wear well if cotton-polyester blend fabrics are used. Cotton broadcloth is appropriate for vests and less frequently laundered garments.

As with other Seminole patchwork projects, the ideal areas to decorate are flat, straight, and stable. Seminole patchwork is suitable for hat bands, epaulets, shirt yokes, dress yokes, overall bibs, apron bibs, vests, cuffs, belts, pockets, pants hems, and skirt hems.

Because of wear and laundering, it is especially important to protect the seam allowances of patchwork used on clothing. Three basic approaches to the construction of Seminole patchwork garments are detailed below.

Topstitched Construction

Patchwork bands may be topstitched onto the garment pieces before sewing the item together. Because the garment piece protects the seam allowances of the patchwork, this is a good method for simple effects on either lined or unlined clothing. Since the patchwork bands with edging strips are only a few inches wide, quilting is usually not necessary.

Many blouse or shirt patterns can be used to make a shirt with Seminole patchwork yokes, and the patchwork orientation can be horizontal, vertical, or angled. Topstitch the patchwork shirt yokes onto the shirt pieces along the bottom edging strip so that the patchwork seam allowances are protected. The patchwork is trimmed to match the shape of the shirt pieces, and all the remaining raw edges are finished off during the construction of the shirt.

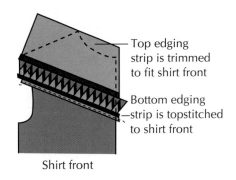

Top edging strip is trimmed to fit shirt front

Bottom edging strip is topstitched to shirt front

Shirt front

Sewing a patchwork yoke to a shirt front

Patchwork bands and edging strips may be sewn together using pattern pieces as guides for size and placement. Cut the garment pieces from this new fabric that is composed of the patchwork. Garments made this way must be lined to protect the seam allowances and may contain a layer of very thin batting or flannel if some padding is desired. Lines of machine quilting every few inches, either decorative or in the seam lines, will secure the layers together. Machine quilting is more appropriate because Seminole patchwork has many layers of seam allowances.

For yokes that are sewn into a garment, use the yoke pattern pieces as guides while sewing patchwork bands and edging strips together. Cut one set of yokes from the patchwork and a second set from lining fabric. Pin a lining to each patchwork yoke and handle as a single layer during the garment construction.

Set-in construction is used when a fabric is either too thin or too heavy to line. The seam allowances of unlined bands need to be finished off with zigzag or serger stitching as the bands are constructed.

To set a straight band of patchwork into a shaped skirt, for example, mark the desired hem length and measure the finished width of the patchwork band. Hem the skirt first, allowing for the width of the patchwork that will be added. Decide how far from the hemline the patchwork will be placed, and mark this measurement all around the skirt. Cut along this line, placing a pin on each side of the cut every 6" (15cm). Sew the patchwork band to each side of the cut. Use the pins as guides for rematching the top and bottom. Finish the seam edges with zigzag or serger stitching.

Topstitched construction can be used to apply patchwork yokes to down vests from kits, with the patchwork topstitched to the ripstop nylon pieces before the vest is sewn.

Patchwork Fabric Construction

The seam allowances in Seminole patchwork can create bulky areas, and some garments will require sturdy edge finishing techniques, such as binding or piping, to produce a smoothly defined garment edge.

Set-In Construction

Cutting line

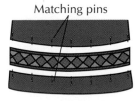

Matching pins

Patchwork band

Cut after hemming

Insert band and sew

Setting a straight patchwork band into a shaped skirt

Design Considerations

The shoulder seam is an important area to consider when planning patchwork yokes. If both the front and back yokes are decorated, plan carefully to keep the shoulder seam area simple.

When the decorative patchwork and edging strips extend high on the yokes, the front design seams may not align with the back seams. To avoid this, the decorated area of each yoke can end at the shoulder, and the yoke area from the shoulder up to the collar can simply be one wide edging strip.

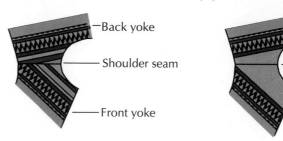

Edging strips too high on yokes | Shoulder seam with wide edging strips

Skirts

Hem areas provide a showcase for designs in Seminole patchwork. Gathered skirts with straight hemlines are the easiest to decorate. Topstitch the patchwork band along the top and bottom edging strips. The skirt itself provides the lining for the patchwork band.

Shaped skirts invite creative solutions because the straight patchwork bands must be made to fit the curve of the skirt hem. Some design bands, particularly those with angle-cut pieces, can be deliberately steamed and pressed into a curve to match the skirt hem. The shaping is done before the edging strips are sewn on, because the top edge will be shorter than the bottom edge. If the curve is great or the edging strips are wide, cut the edging strips on the bias. Topstitch the edged band onto the skirt.

To set a patchwork band into a skirt, see the previous section, "Set-in Construction."

Design bands can be shaped into a curve as the band is being constructed. Sew a generous 1/4" (0.6cm) seam allowance at the top of the pieces and a scant 1/4" (0.6cm) at the bottom. When the correct curve is achieved, attach bias-cut edging strips and topstitch onto the skirt.

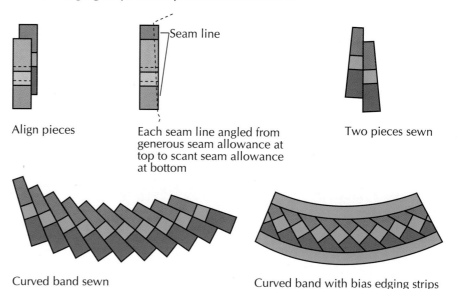

Align pieces

Each seam line angled from generous seam allowance at top to scant seam allowance at bottom

Two pieces sewn

Curved band sewn

Curved band with bias edging strips

Sewing a curve into a patchwork band for a shaped skirt

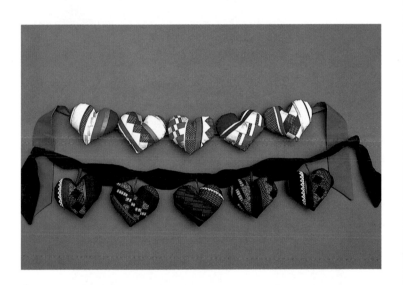

Quilts

Seminole patchwork bands used as sashing and borders showcase quilt blocks and frame quilt designs. You can make fabulous quilts using the designs in this book.

The quilts "Kilim" and "Directions" show examples of Seminole patchwork used to turn corners. Design help can be found in the section on Pieces Turning Corners in Chapter 6. If you prefer to spend less time piecing, use plain blocks in the corners as shown in the "Alligator" quilt. "Scheherazade" and "Peace Flower" avoid turning patchwork corners by using plain strips to separate the patchwork borders.

Sashings and borders made from Seminole patchwork may vary in size. To plan correctly, first sew the patchwork bands, measure their final size, and then plan the dimensions for the layout of your quilt top.

Adjust the scale of designs to make them work in your quilt. Miniaturized Seminole designs are integral to the small quilts on page 32. An alternate design for the squares in "Nine-patch" would be to place them straight as opposed to placing them at an angle. The quilt "Directions" utilizes a strong border created by enlarging Design 3.

Seminole patchwork creates many layers of seam allowances making it necessary to machine quilt. Pin baste with 1" safety pins to prepare for machine quilting. The quilting can be sewn with a strong polyester sewing thread in colors that match or contrast with the quilt top. Use one bobbin thread color that blends with the quilt back fabric. Quilting lines which follow the seam lines or form decorative straight line designs can be sewn with a normal presser foot. Free form quilting is done with a darning foot and dropped feed dog. Machine quilting results in many thread ends to be tied off on the back. A busy print used for the quilt back will help to hide the knots.

Detail of the "Alligator" quilt showing free form machine quilting

A delightful print fabric is contained in a border of patchwork bands of Design 7 in the Alligator Quilt by Virginia Schnalle. The outer border, a variation of Design 7, has corner blocks constructed from a variation of Design 8. All the quilting, including the stippled effect on the print fabric, is machine quilting.

These miniature quilts, by the author, are each about 8" x 10" (20 x 25cm). "Amish Bricks" (left) is a variation of Design 15. The center strip is composed of 6" (15cm) sections of seven different colors butted together. "Sawtooth Diamond" (middle) has half-scale bands of Design 32 sewn around the central square and on the borders. "Nine-patch" (left) is a one-third scale variation of Design 50.

"Peace Flower," a wall hanging by the author, has Seminole patchwork bands for borders, alternating with plain border strips. The patchwork bands used are a variation of Design 6 and a half-scale Design 1 and 11. The center motif is a machine applique.

"Kilim," a wall hanging by the author, carries the patchwork designs through the corners of the borders. This overall design and the fabric choice of cotton velveteen made this a challenging project. The inner motifs are mirror image bands of Design 29 sewn around diamond-shaped centers. The two outer borders are a variation of Design 17, and a double-scale variation of Design 43, with the narrowest strips in two different colors.

Striking colors and Seminole patchwork bands turning corners create "Directions," a contemporary wall hanging by Penny Nii. Designs 2, 3, 5 and 18 were used.

"Scheherazade," by the author, measures 18" x 24" (46 x 61cm). It has a machine-appliqued, hand-beaded, and hand-quilted center block. The borders alternate Seminole patchwork bands with plain strips, creating a simple effect without patchwork designs converging at the corners. The patchwork bands used are Designs 6 and 11, with a variation of Design 11.

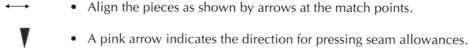

5. Seminole Design Diagrams

Selection of an Appropriate Design Diagram

The design diagrams are presented in order of increasing complexity. If you are a beginner, start with Design 1. If you are experienced, begin anywhere and have fun.

Estimating Yardage

For experimenting with Seminole designs, 1/4 yard (0.25m) of each color for each design is a practical amount of fabric to purchase. Any extra fabric can be used for edging strips and for trying out the unexpected color combinations that will present themselves as you work with the fabrics. When planning a specific project, the approximate Finished Band Size given in each design diagram is an aid to estimating yardage. Add up the widths of the strips to be cut from each color to determine the minimum yardage needed, and then add some extra for the edging strips and loss to prewashing and trimming.

Changing the Scale of a Design

The scale of designs in the diagrams will work well for the projects in Chapter 4. The designs often work well together, so try combining several designs for a tote bag pocket or a book cover. If you wish to adjust the scale of a design, follow the steps below.

Step 1. Determine the original finished size by subtracting the two 1/4" (0.6cm) seam allowances from the strip widths *and* piece widths in the design diagram. For angle-cut pieces made using a ruler without angle markings, subtract from the measurement marks instead of from the piece widths. (See Method One in Chapter 3). You are left with the original finished size.

Step 2. Choose a convenient number to scale the original finished size up or down, using the approximate desired size as a guide. The minimum finished size used in this book is 1/4" (0.6cm), so it is not recommended that you attempt to scale down designs already containing that measurement.

Step 3. Add the two 1/4" (0.6cm) seam allowances back onto both the strip widths and the piece widths. There is no need to change the size of the seam allowance, regardless of the size of the patchwork.

Reading the Design Diagrams

- The strip width and piece width measurements in the diagrams are the cutting size. Seam allowances have already been added.

- Seam allowances of 1/4" (0.6cm) are used throughout.

- Measurements in the design diagrams are offered in inches or centimeters. These measurements are *not* interchangeable, so choose one system to use.

- Special techniques that apply to a design are noted in the diagrams.

- Measurements under Final Band Size give the approximate width and length of the finished patchwork band. It is assumed that the design is sewn using one set of 42" (105cm) long strips.

- Align the pieces as shown by arrows at the match points.

- A pink arrow indicates the direction for pressing seam allowances.

- A green box surrounds a complete design unit for designs made up of nonidentical pieces.

Finished Band Size: 1-1/4" (3cm) wide, 36" (86cm) long

Measurements in the design diagrams are offered in inches or centimeters. These measurements are not interchangeable, so choose one system to use.

Step 1:
Cut the strips.

1-1/2" (3.6cm)

1-1/4" (3cm)

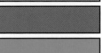
1-1/2" (3.6cm)

Step 2:
Sew the strip set.
Press.

Step 3:
Cut the pieces.

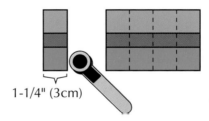

1-1/4" (3cm)

Step 4:
Align the pieces and sew together.
Press.

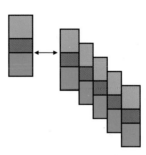

Step 5:
Mark lines for the edging strips
(page 17).

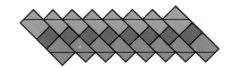

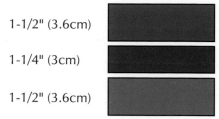

Design 2
Straight-Cut, Upside Down

Finished Band Size: 1-1/4" (3cm) wide, 36" (86cm) long

Step 1:
Cut the strips.

1-1/2" (3.6cm)

1-1/4" (3cm)

1-1/2" (3.6cm)

Step 2:
Sew the strip set.
Press.

Step 3:
Cut the pieces.
Turn half of the a. pieces upside down to get the b. pieces.

a.

b.

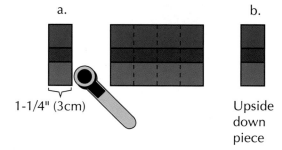

1-1/4" (3cm)

Upside down piece

Step 4:
Align the pieces and sew together.
Seam allowances will butt.
Press.

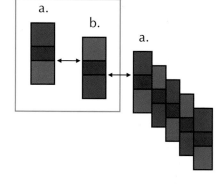

a.

b.

a.

Step 5:
Mark lines for the edging strips (page 17).

Finished Band Size: 2" (4.8cm) wide, 32" (77cm) long

Step 1:
Cut the strips.

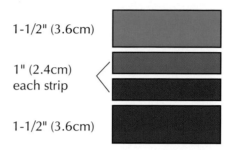

1-1/2" (3.6cm)

1" (2.4cm)
each strip

1-1/2" (3.6cm)

Step 2:
Sew the strip set.
Press.

Step 3:
Cut the pieces.

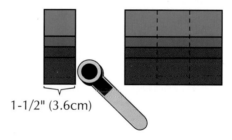

1-1/2" (3.6cm)

Step 4:
Align the pieces and sew together.
Press.

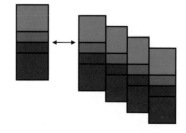

Step 5:
Mark lines for the edging strips
(page 17).

Design 4
Straight-Cut

Finished Band Size: 2-3/4" (6.6cm) wide, 36" (86cm) long

Step 1:
Cut the strips.

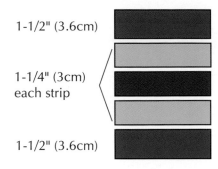

1-1/2" (3.6cm)

1-1/4" (3cm)
each strip

1-1/2" (3.6cm)

Step 2:
Sew the strip set.
Press.

Step 3:
Cut the pieces.

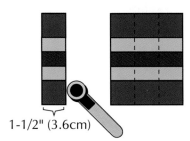

1-1/2" (3.6cm)

Step 4:
Align the pieces and sew together.
Press.

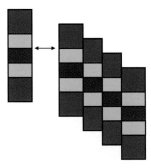

Step 5:
Mark lines for the edging strips
(page 17).

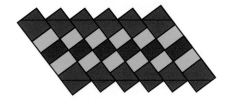

Finished Band Size: 3" (7.2cm) wide, 36" (86cm) long

This design can be made any size. The outside strips are cut 1/4" (0.6cm) wider than the inside strips. The pieces are cut the same width as the inside strips.

Step 1:
Cut the strips.

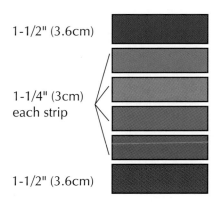

1-1/2" (3.6cm)

1-1/4" (3cm) each strip

1-1/2" (3.6cm)

Step 2:
Sew the strip set. Press.

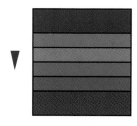

Step 3:
Cut the pieces.

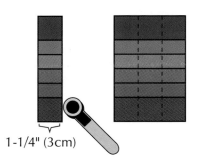

1-1/4" (3cm)

Step 4:
Align the pieces and sew together. Press.

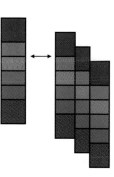

Step 5:
Mark lines for the edging strips (page 17).

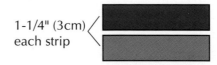

Design 6
Straight-Cut, Upside Down

Finished Band Size: 1-1/2" (3.6cm) wide, 26" (62cm) long

Step 1:
Cut the strips.

1-1/4" (3cm) each strip

Step 2:
Sew the strip set.
Press.

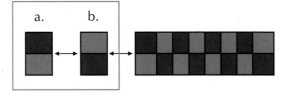

Step 3:
Cut the pieces.
Turn half of the a. pieces upside down to make the b. pieces.

a.   b.

1-1/4" (3cm)

Upside down piece

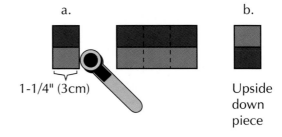

Step 4:
Align the pieces and sew together.
Seam allowances will butt.
Press.

a.   b.

Step 5:
The edges of the patchwork band are used as the placement lines for the edging strips.

Finished Band Size: 1-3/4" (4.2cm) wide, 28" (67cm) long

Design 7
Straight-Cut, Upside Down

Step 1:
Cut the strips.

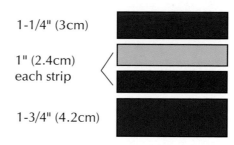

1-1/4" (3cm)

1" (2.4cm)
each strip

1-3/4" (4.2cm)

Step 2:
Sew the strip set.
Press.

Step 3:
Cut the pieces.
Turn half of the a. pieces upside
down to make the b. pieces.

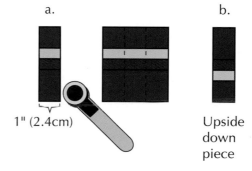

a.

b.

1" (2.4cm)

Upside
down
piece

Step 4:
Align the pieces and sew together.
Seam allowances will butt.
Press.

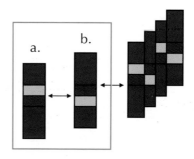

a.

b.

Step 5:
Mark lines for the edging strips
(page 17).

Design 8
Straight-Cut, Multiple Strip Sets

Finished Band Size: 2-1/2" (6cm) wide, 42" (101cm) long

Step 1:
Cut the strips.

a.

b.

1" (2.4cm)
each strip

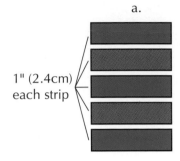

1-1/2" (3.6cm)

1" (2.4cm)

1-1/2" (3.6cm)

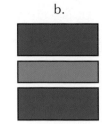

Step 2:
Sew the strip sets.
Press.

a.

b.

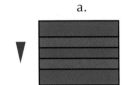

Step 3:
Cut the pieces.

a.

b.

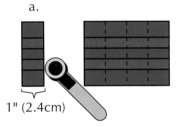

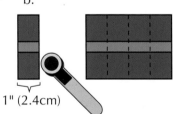

1" (2.4cm)

1" (2.4cm)

Step 4:
Align the pieces and sew together.
Seam allowances will butt.
Press.

a.   b.

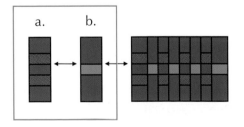

Step 5:
The edges of the patchwork band
are used as the placement lines
for the edging strips.

Finished Band Size: 2-1/2" (6cm) wide, 42" (101cm) long

Design 9
Straight-Cut, Multiple Strip Sets

Step 1:
Cut the strips.

a.

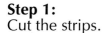

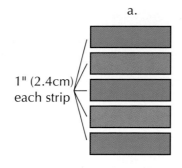

1" (2.4cm)
each strip

1-1/2" (3.6cm)

1" (2.4cm)

1-1/2" (3.6cm)

b.

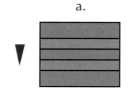

c.

1" (2.5cm)

Step 2:
Sew the strip sets.
Press.

a.

b.

Step 3:
Cut the pieces.
(Only half of the b. pieces
will be used.)

a.

b.

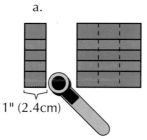

1" (2.4cm)

1" (2.4cm)

c.

3" (7.2cm)

Step 4:
Align the pieces and sew together.
Seam allowances will butt.
Press.

a.   b.   a.   c.

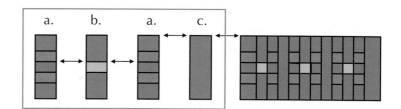

Step 5:
The edges of the patchwork band
are used as the placement lines for
the edging strips.

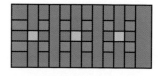

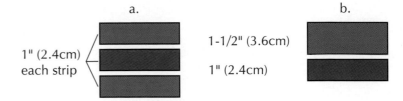

Design 10

**Straight-Cut, Multiple Strip Sets,
Upside Down**

Finished Band Size: 1-1/2" (3.6cm) wide, 42" (101cm) long

Step 1:
Cut the strips.

a.

1" (2.4cm)
each strip

1-1/2" (3.6cm)

1" (2.4cm)

b.

Step 2:
Sew the strip sets.
Press.

a.

b.

Step 3:
Cut the pieces.
Turn half of the b. pieces upside
down to make the c. pieces.

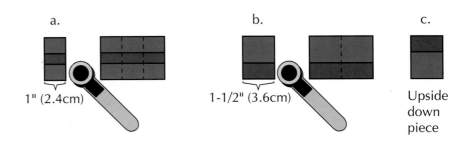

a.

1" (2.4cm)

b.

1-1/2" (3.6cm)

c.

Upside
down
piece

Step 4:
Align the pieces and sew together.
Some seam allowances will butt.
Press.

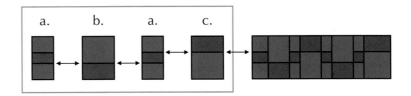

a. b. a. c.

Step 5:
The edges of the patchwork band
are used as the placement lines
for the edging strips.

Finished Band Size: 1" (2.4cm) wide, 40" (96cm) long

This design can be made any size. The strips are cut 3/4" (1.8cm) wider than the finished width of the pieces. The offset distance always equals the finished width of the pieces.

Step 1:
Cut the strips.

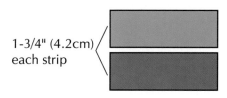

1-3/4" (4.2cm) each strip

Step 2:
Sew the strip set.
Press.

Step 3:
Mark strip set with offset line (page 19).

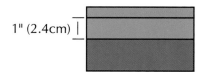

1" (2.4cm)

Step 4:
Cut the pieces.

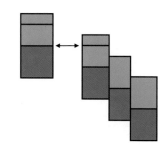

1-1/2" (3.6cm)

Step 5:
Align the pieces and sew together.
Press.

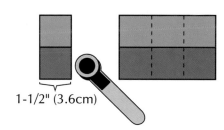

Step 6:
Mark lines for the edging strips (page 17).

Design 12
Straight Cut, Offset

Finished Band Size: 1-3/4" (4.2cm) wide, 20" (48cm) long

Follow steps 1–5 in Design 11.

Step 6:
Remove a seam in the middle of the patchwork band, making two separate bands.

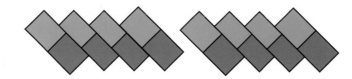

Step 7:
Cut along the lines shown, 1/4" (0.6cm) outside the design points.

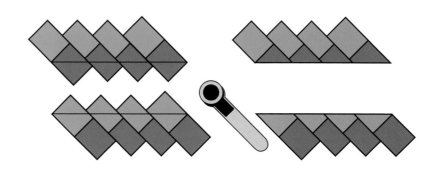

Step 8:
Align the bands and sew together, using pins at the design points.

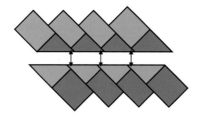

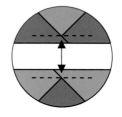

Enlarged view
of alignment

Step 9:
Press.

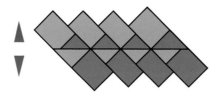

Step 10:
Mark lines for the edging strips (page 17).

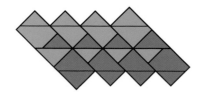

Finished Band Size: 1-3/4" (4.2cm) wide, 20" (48cm) long

Design 13
Straight Cut, Offset

Follow steps 1–5 in Design 11.

Step 6:
Remove a seam in the middle of the patchwork band, making two separate bands.

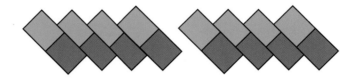

Step 7:
Cut along the lines shown, 1/4" (0.6cm) outside the design points.

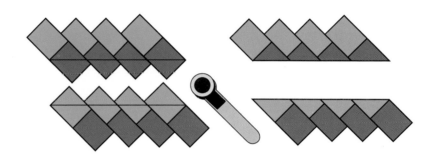

Step 8:
Align the bands and sew together.

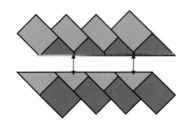

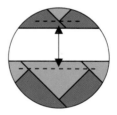

Enlarged view
of alignment

Step 9:
Press.

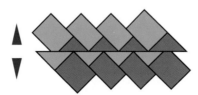

Step 10:
Mark lines for the edging strips (page 17).

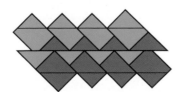

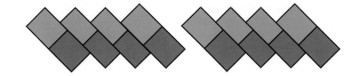

Design 14
Straight Cut, Offset

Finished Band Size: 1-3/4" (4.2cm) wide, 20" (48cm) long

Follow steps 1–5 in Design 11.

Step 6:
Remove a seam in the middle of the patchwork band, making two separate bands.

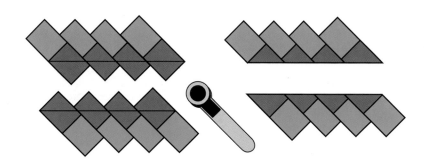

Step 7:
Cut along the lines shown, 1/4" (0.6cm) outside the design points.

Step 8:
Align the bands and sew together.

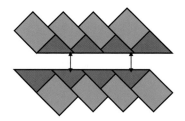
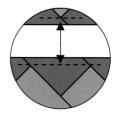

Enlarged view of alignment

Step 9:
Press.

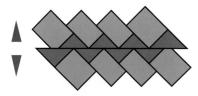

Step 10:
Mark lines for the edging strips (page 17).

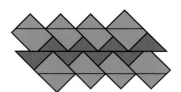

Finished Band Size: 1-3/4" (4.2cm) wide, 28" (67cm) long

Design 15
Straight-Cut, Offset

Step 1:
Cut the strips.

1-1/4" (3cm)

1-3/4" (4.2cm)

1-1/4" (3cm)

Step 2:
Sew the strip set.
Press.

Step 3:
Mark strip set with offset line
(page 19).

1/2" (1.2cm)

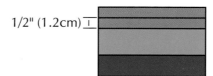

Step 4:
Cut the pieces.

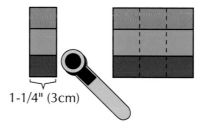

1-1/4" (3cm)

Step 5:
Align the pieces and sew together.
Press.

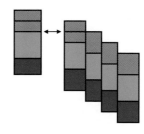

Step 6:
Mark lines for the edging strips
(page 17).

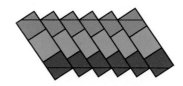

Design 16
Straight-Cut, Offset, Upside Down

Finished Band Size: 1-1/4" (3cm) wide, 33" (79cm) long

Step 1:
Cut the strips.

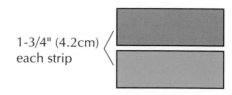

1-3/4" (4.2cm)
each strip

Step 2:
Sew the strip set.
Press.

Step 3:
Mark strip set with two offset lines
(page 19).

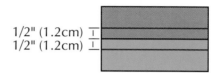

1/2" (1.2cm)
1/2" (1.2cm)

Step 4:
Cut the pieces.
Turn half of the a. pieces upside
down to make the b. pieces.

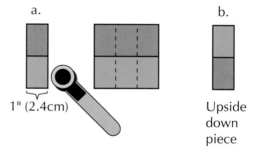

a.

b.

1" (2.4cm)

Upside
down
piece

Step 5:
Align the pieces and sew together.
Press.

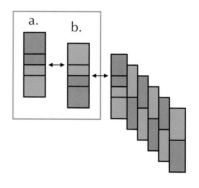

a. b.

Step 6:
Mark lines for the edging strips
(page 17).

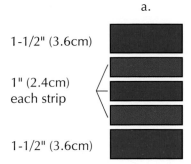

Finished Band Size: 2" (4.8cm) wide, 56" (134cm) long

Step 1:
Cut the strips.

a.

b.

1-1/2" (3.6cm)

1" (2.4cm)
each strip

1-1/2" (3.6cm)

Cut 4 strips:
1" (2.4cm)

Step 2:
Sew strip set a.
Press.

a.

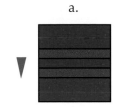

Step 3:
Cut the a. pieces
Cut the b. pieces and mark offset
line (page 19) 1/2" (1.2cm) from
one end of each b. piece.

a.

1" (2.4cm)

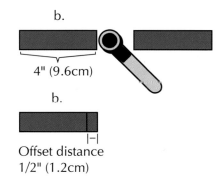

b.

4" (9.6cm)

b.

Offset distance
1/2" (1.2cm)

Step 4:
Align the pieces and sew
together.
Press.

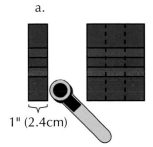

a. b.

Step 5:
Mark lines for the edging strips
(page 17).

Design 18

Finished Band Size: 1-1/2" (3.6cm) wide, 40" (96cm) long

Straight-Cut, Multiple Strip Sets, Offset

Step 1:
Cut the strips.

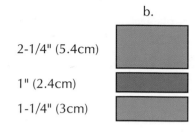
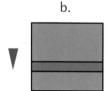

a.

1-1/4" (3cm)

1" (2.4cm)
each strip

1-1/4" (3cm)

b.

2-1/4" (5.4cm)

1" (2.4cm)

1-1/4" (3cm)

Step 2:
Sew the strip sets.
Press.

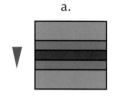
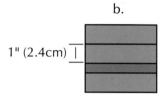

a.

b.

Step 3:
Mark strip set b. with offset line
(page 19).

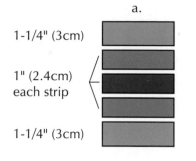

b.

1" (2.4cm)

Step 4:
Cut the a. pieces.
(Only half of the a. pieces will be used.)
Cut the b. pieces.
Turn half of the b. pieces upside down
to make the c. pieces.

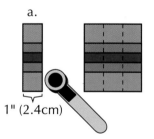
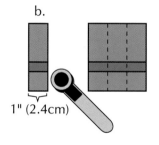

a.

1" (2.4cm)

b.

1" (2.4cm)

c.

Upside
down
piece

Step 5:
Align the pieces and sew together.

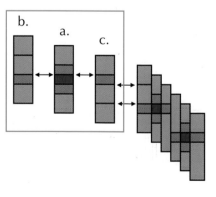

b.

a.

c.

Step 6:
Mark lines for the edging strips
(page 17).

Finished Band Size: 1-1/2" (3.6cm) wide, 50" (120cm) long

Straight-Cut, Multiple Strip Sets, Offset

Step 1:
Cut the strips.

a.

1-1/4" (3cm)

1" (2.4cm)
each strip

1-1/4" (3cm)

b.

2-1/4" (5.4cm)

1" (2.4cm)

1-1/4" (3cm)

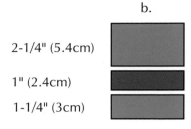

Step 2:
Sew the strip sets.
Press.

a. 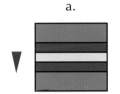 b.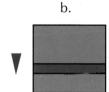

Step 3:
Mark strip set b. with offset line
(page 19).

b.

1" (2.4cm)

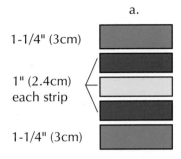

Step 4:
Cut the a. pieces.
Cut the b. pieces.
Turn half of the b. pieces upside
down to make the c. pieces.

a. b. c.

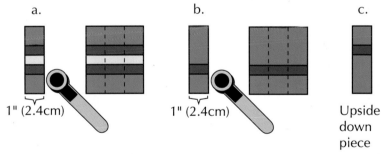

1" (2.4cm) 1" (2.4cm) Upside
down
piece

Step 5:
Align the pieces and sew together.

Step 6:
Mark lines for the edging strips
(page 17).

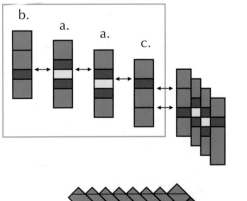

Design 20
Straight-Cut, 3/4" Strips

Finished Band Size: 1-1/2" (3.6cm) wide, 33" (79cm) long

Step 1:
Cut the strips.

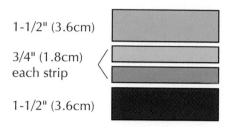

1-1/2" (3.6cm)

3/4" (1.8cm)
each strip

1-1/2" (3.6cm)

Step 2:
Sew the strip set, using the 3/4" Strip Technique where appropriate (page 18).
Press.

Step 3:
Cut the pieces.

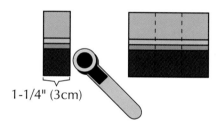

1-1/4" (3cm)

Step 4:
Align the pieces and sew together.

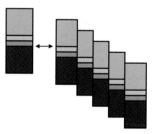

Step 5:
Mark lines for the edging strips (page 17).

Finished Band Size: 1-3/4" (4.2cm) wide, 32" (77cm) long

Step 1:
Cut the strips.

1-1/2" (3.6cm)

3/4" (1.8cm)

1-1/4" (3cm)

3/4" (1.8cm)

1-1/2" (3.6cm)

Step 2:
Sew the strip set, using the
3/4" Strip Technique where
appropriate (page 18).
Press.

Step 3:
Cut the pieces.

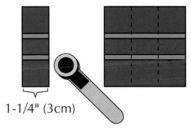

1-1/4" (3cm)

Step 4:
Align the pieces and sew together.

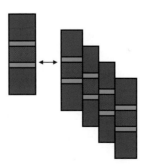

Step 5:
Mark lines for the edging strips
(page 17).

Design 22
Straight-Cut, 3/4" Strips

Finished Band Size: 1-1/4" (3cm) wide, 36" (86cm) long

Step 1:
Cut the strips.

1-3/4" (4.2cm)

3/4" (1.8cm)

1" (2.4cm)

3/4" (1.8cm)

1-3/4" (4.2cm)

Step 2:
Sew the strip set, using the
3/4" Strip Technique where
appropriate (page 18).
Press.

Step 3:
Cut the pieces.

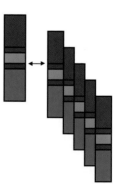

1" (2.4cm)

Step 4:
Align the pieces and sew together.

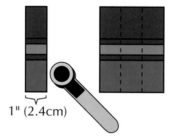

Step 5:
Mark lines for the edging strips
(page 17).

Finished Band Size: 1-1/4" (3cm) wide, 33" (79cm) long

Design 23

Straight-Cut, Upside Down, 3/4" Strips

Step 1:
Cut the strips.

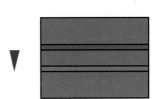

1-1/2" (3.6cm)

3/4" (1.8cm)

1-1/4" (3cm)

3/4" (1.8cm)

1-1/2" (3.6cm)

Step 2:
Sew the strip set, using the
3/4" Strip Technique where
appropriate (page 18).
Press.

Step 3:
Cut the pieces.
Turn half of the a. pieces upside
down to make the b. pieces.

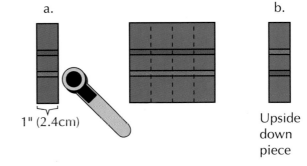

a.

1" (2.4cm)

b.

Upside
down
piece

Step 4:
Align the pieces and sew together.
Seam allowances will butt.
Press.

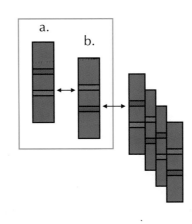

a.

b.

Step 5:
Mark lines for the edging strips
(page 17).

Design 24

Straight-Cut, Upside Down, 3/4" Strip

Finished Band Size: 2-1/4" (5.4cm) wide, 28" (67cm) long

Step 1:
Cut the strips.

1-1/2" (3.6cm)

1-1/4" (3cm)

1" (2.4cm)

3/4" (1.8cm)

2" (4.8cm)

Step 2:
Sew the strip set, using the 3/4" Strip Technique where appropriate (page 18).
Press.

Step 3:
Cut the pieces.
Turn half of the a. pieces upside down to make the b. pieces.

a.

b.

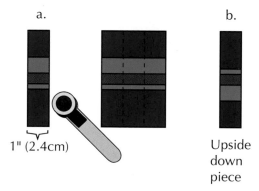

1" (2.4cm)

Upside down piece

Step 4:
Align the pieces and sew together.
Seam allowances will butt.
Press.

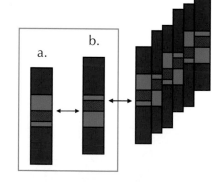

a.

b.

Step 5:
Mark lines for the edging strips (page 17).

Finished Band Size: 2" (4.8cm) wide, 36" (86cm) long

Design 25
Straight-Cut, Upside Down, 3/4" Strips

Step 1:
Cut the strips.

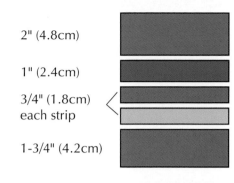

2" (4.8cm)

1" (2.4cm)

3/4" (1.8cm)
each strip

1-3/4" (4.2cm)

Step 2:
Sew the strip set, using the
3/4" Strip Technique where
appropriate (page 18).
Press.

Step 3:
Cut the pieces.
Turn half of the a. pieces upside
down to make the b. pieces.

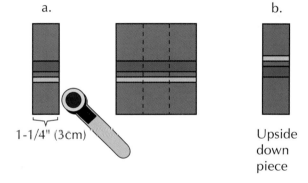

a.

b.

1-1/4" (3cm)

Upside
down
piece

Step 4:
Align the pieces and sew together.
Seam allowances will butt.
Press.

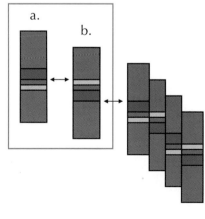

a.

b.

Step 5:
Mark lines for the edging strips
(page 17).

Design 26

Finished Band Size: 2-1/4" (5.4cm) wide, 44" (106cm) long

Straight-Cut, Upside Down, 3/4" Strips

Step 1:
Cut the strips.

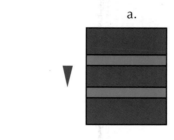

a.

1-1/2" (3.6cm)

1" (2.4cm)

1-1/2" (3.6cm)

1" (2.4cm)

1-1/2" (3.6cm)

b.

2-1/4" (5.4cm)

3/4" (1.8cm)

2-1/4" (5.4cm)

Step 2:
Sew strip set a.
Sew strip set b., using the
3/4" Strip Technique where
appropriate (page 18).
Press.

Step 3:
Cut the pieces.

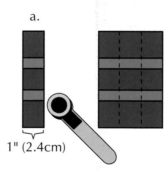

a.

1" (2.4cm)

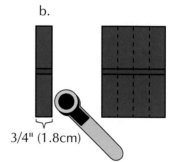

b.

3/4" (1.8cm)

Step 4:
Align the pieces and sew together.
Seam allowances will butt.
Press.

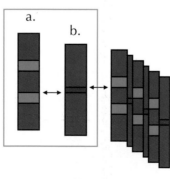

a.

b.

Step 5:
Mark lines for the edging strips
(page 17).

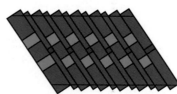

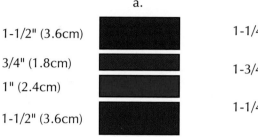

Finished Band Size: 1-3/4" (4.2cm) wide, 34" (82cm) long

Design 27

Straight-Cut, Upside Down, 3/4" Strips

Step 1:

Cut the strips.

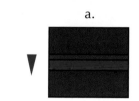 a.

1-1/2" (3.6cm)

3/4" (1.8cm)

1" (2.4cm)

1-1/2" (3.6cm)

b.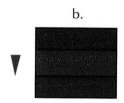

1-1/4" (3cm)

1-3/4" (4.2cm)

1-1/4" (3cm)

Step 2:

Sew strip set a., using the 3/4" Strip Technique where appropriate (page 18). Sew strip set b. Press.

a.

b.

Step 3:

Cut the a. pieces. Turn half of the a. pieces upside down to make the c. pieces. Cut the b. pieces.

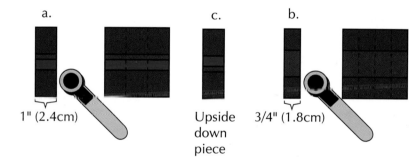

a.   c.   b.

1" (2.4cm)   Upside   3/4" (1.8cm)
                  down
                  piece

Step 4:

Align the pieces and sew together, using the 3/4" Strip Technique where appropriate (page 18). Some seam allowances will butt. Press.

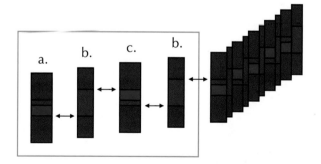

a.   b.   c.   b.

Step 5:

Mark lines for the edging strips (page 17).

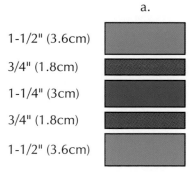

Design 28
Straight-Cut, Offset, 3/4" Strips

Finished Band Size: 1-3/4" (4.2cm) wide, 48" (115cm) long

Step 1:
Cut the strips.

a.

1-1/2" (3.6cm)

3/4" (1.8cm)

1-1/4" (3cm)

3/4" (1.8cm)

1-1/2" (3.6cm)

b.

Cut 3 strips:
3/4" (1.8cm)

Step 2:
Sew strip set a., using the
3/4" Strip Technique where
appropriate (page 18).
Press.

a.

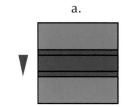

Step 3:
Cut the a. pieces.
Cut the b. pieces, and mark
offset line (page 19) 1/2"
(1.2cm) from one end of each
b. piece.

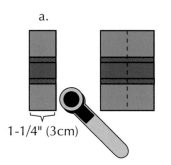

a.

1-1/4" (3cm)

b.

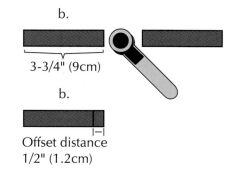

3-3/4" (9cm)

b.

Offset distance
1/2" (1.2cm)

Step 4:
Align the pieces and sew together.
Press.

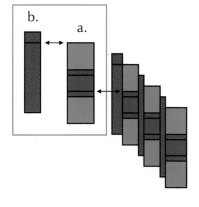

b.

a.

Step 5:
Mark lines for the edging strips
(page 17).

Finished Band Size: 1-1/4" (3cm) wide, 18" (43cm) long

Design 29
Angle-Cut

Step 1:
Cut the strips.

1-1/2" (3.6cm) each strip

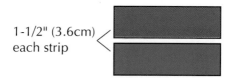

Step 2:
Sew the strip set.
Press.

Step 3:
Cut the pieces using either Method One (page 13) or Method Two (page 14).

Method One

3" (7.5cm) 2" (5cm)

Zero point

2" (5cm) 2" (5cm)

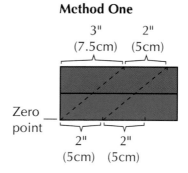

Method Two
45° angle and 1-1/4" (3cm) wide

Step 4:
Align the pieces and sew together.
Press.

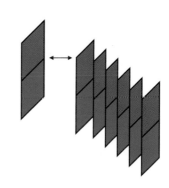

Step 5:
Mark lines for the edging strips (page 17).

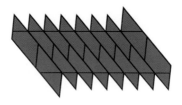

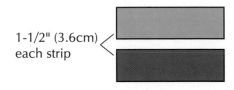

Design 30
Angle-Cut, Upside Down

Finished Band Size: 1-1/4" (3cm) wide, 16" (38cm) long

Step 1:
Cut the strips.

1-1/2" (3.6cm) each strip

Step 2:
Sew the strip set.
Press.

Step 3:
Cut the pieces using either Method One (page 13) or Method Two (page 14). Turn half of the a. pieces upside down to make the b. pieces.

Method One

2-1/2" 1-1/2"
(6cm) (3.5cm)

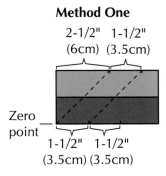

Zero point

1-1/2" 1-1/2"
(3.5cm) (3.5cm)

Method Two
45° angle and 1-1/4" (3cm) wide

a.

b.

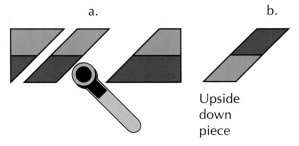

Upside down piece

Step 4:
Align the pieces and sew together.
Press.

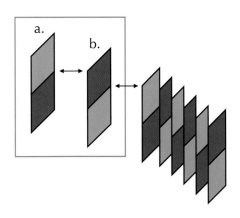

Step 5:
Mark lines for the edging strips (page 17).

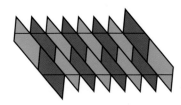

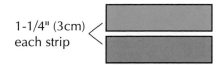

Finished Band Size: 1-1/2" (3.6cm) wide, 22" (53cm) long

Design 31
Angle-Cut, Upside Down

Step 1:
Cut the strips.

1-1/4" (3cm)
each strip

Step 2:
Sew the strip
set.

Step 3:
Cut the pieces using
either Method One (page
13) or Method Two (page
14).
Turn half of the a. pieces
upside down to make the

Method One

2-1/2" 1-1/2"
(6cm) (3.5cm)

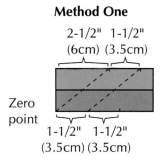

Zero
point

1-1/2" 1-1/2"
(3.5cm) (3.5cm)

Method Two
45° angle and 1" (2.4cm) wide

a.

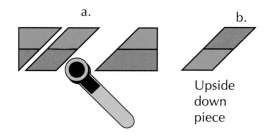

b.

Upside
down
piece

Step 4:
Align the pieces and pin at the
match points on the sewing
lines, rather than on the edges
of the pieces.
Sew together.
Press.

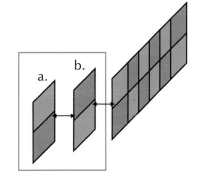

a.

b.

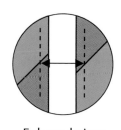

Enlarged view
of alignment

Step 5:
The edges of the patchwork
band are used as the placement
lines for the edging strips.

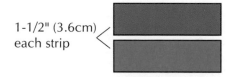

Design 32
Angle-Cut, Offset

Finished Band Size: 1-1/4" (3cm) wide, 26" (62cm) long

Step 1:
Cut the strips.

1-1/2" (3.6cm)
each strip

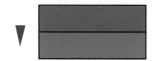

Step 2:
Sew the strip set.
Press.

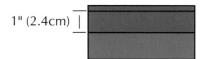

Step 3:
Mark the strip set with offset line
(page 19).

1" (2.4cm)

Step 4:
Cut the pieces using either
Method One (page 13) or
Method Two (page 14).

Method One

1-1/2"   1-1/2"
(3.5cm) (3.5cm)

Zero
point

1-1/2"   1-1/2"
(3.5cm) (3.5cm)

Method Two
60° angle and 1-1/4" (3cm) wide

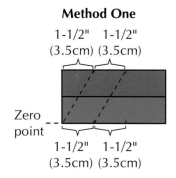

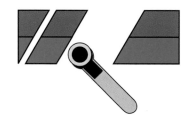

Step 5:
Align the pieces and sew together.
Press.

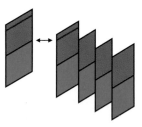

Step 6:
Mark lines for the edging strips
(page 17).

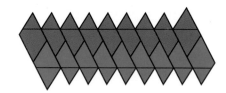

Finished Band Size: 2-1/2" (6cm) wide, 16" (38cm) long

Design 33
Angle-Cut

Step 1:
Cut the strips.

1-1/2" (3.6cm)

1-1/4" (3cm)

1-1/2" (3.6cm)

Step 2:
Sew the strip set.
Press.

Step 3:
Cut the pieces using either
Method One (page 13) or
Method Two (page 14).

Method One

3-1/2"   1-3/4"
(8.5cm)   (4.5cm)

Zero
point

1-3/4"   1-3/4"
(4.5cm)   (4.5cm)

Method Two
45° angle and 1-1/4" (3cm) wide

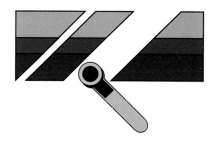

Step 4:
Align the pieces and pin at the
match points on the sewing lines,
rather than on the edges of the
pieces.
Sew together.
Press.

Enlarged view
of alignment

Step 5:
Mark lines for the edging strips
(page 17).

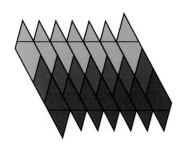

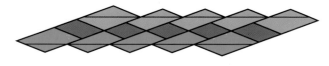

Design 34
Angle-Cut

Finished Band Size: 1" (2.4cm) wide, 35" (84cm) long

Step 1:
Cut the strips.

1-1/2" (3.6cm)

1-1/4" (3cm)

1-1/2" (3.6cm)

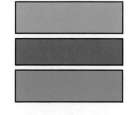

Step 2:
Sew the strip set.
Press.

Step 3:
Cut the pieces using either
Method One (page 13) or
Method Two (page 14).

Method One

3-1/2"   1-3/4"
(8.5cm)   (4.5cm)

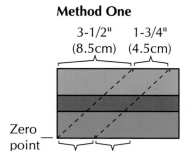

Zero
point

1-3/4" 1-3/4"
(4.5cm)(4.5cm)

Method Two
45° angle and 1-1/4" (3cm) wide

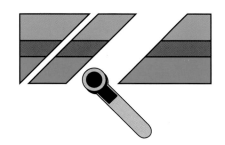

Step 4:
Align the pieces and pin at the
match points on the sewing lines,
rather than on the edges of the
pieces.
Sew together.
Press.

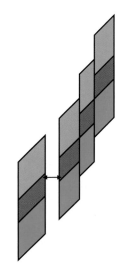

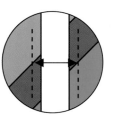

Enlarged view
of alignment

Step 5:
Mark lines for the edging strips
(page 17).

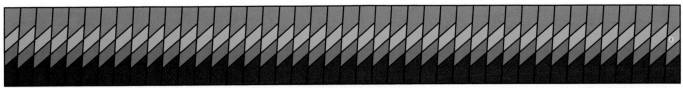

Finished Band Size: 3-1/2" (8.4cm) wide, 13" (31cm) long

Design 35
Angle-Cut

Step 1:
Cut the strips.

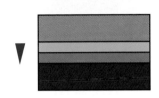

1-1/2" (3.6cm)

1" (2.4cm)
each strip

1-1/2" (3.6cm)

Step 2:
Sew the strip set.
Press.

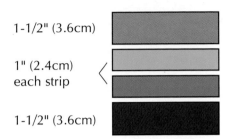

Step 3:
Cut the pieces using either
Method One (page 13) or
Method Two (page 14).

Method One

3-1/2"   1-3/4"
(8.5cm) (4.5cm)

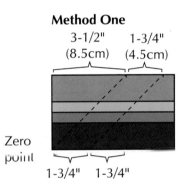

Zero
point

1-3/4" 1-3/4"
(4.5cm) (4.5cm)

Method Two
45° angle and 1-1/4" (3cm) wide

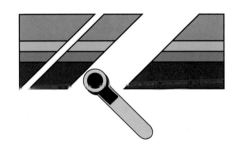

Step 4:
Align the pieces and pin at the
match points on the sewing lines,
rather than on the edges of the
pieces.
Sew together.
Press.

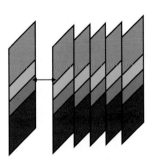

Enlarged view
of alignment

Step 5:
Mark lines for the edging strips
(page 17).

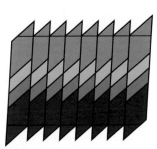

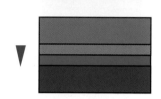

Design 36
Angle-Cut

Step 1:
Cut the strips.

1-1/2" (3.6cm)

1" (2.4cm)
each strip

1-1/2" (3.6cm)

Step 2:
Sew the strip set.
Press.

Step 3:
Cut the pieces using either
Method One (page 13) or
Method Two (page 14).

Method One

3-1/2"   1-3/4"
(8.5cm)   (4.5cm)

Zero
point

1-3/4"   1-3/4"
(4.5cm) (4.5cm)

Method Two
45° angle and 1-1/4" (3cm) wide

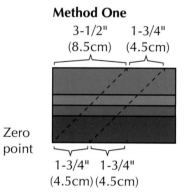

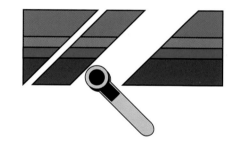

Step 4:
Align the pieces and pin at the
match points on the sewing lines,
rather than on the edges of the
pieces.
Sew together.
Press.

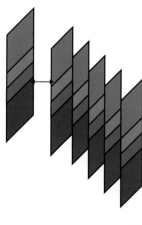

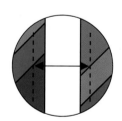

Enlarged view
of alignment

Step 5:
Mark lines for the edging strips
(page 17).

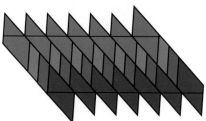

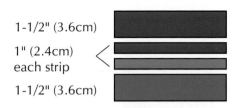

Finished Band Size: 1-1/4" (3cm) wide, 30" (72cm) long

Step 1:
Cut the strips.

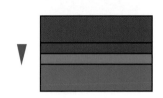

1-1/2" (3.6cm)

1" (2.4cm)
each strip

1-1/2" (3.6cm)

Step 2:
Sew the strip set.
Press.

Step 3:
Cut the pieces using either
Method One (page 13) or
Method Two (page 14).

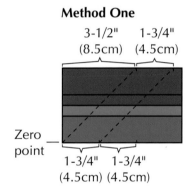

Method One

3-1/2"   1-3/4"
(8.5cm)   (4.5cm)

Zero
point

1-3/4"   1-3/4"
(4.5cm) (4.5cm)

Method Two
45° angle and 1-1/4" (3cm) wide

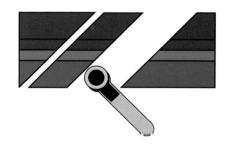

Step 4:
Align the pieces and pin at the
match points on the sewing lines,
rather than on the edges of the
pieces.
Sew together.
Press.

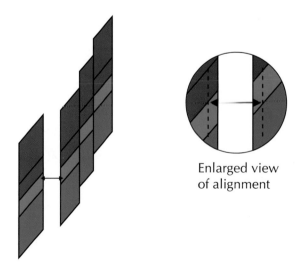

Enlarged view
of alignment

Step 5:
Mark lines for the edging strips
(page 17).

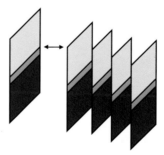

Design 38

Angle-Cut, 3/4" Strip

Finished Band Size: 2" (5cm) wide, 18" (43cm) long

Step 1:
Cut the strips.

1-1/2" (3.6cm)

3/4" (1.8cm)

1-1/2" (3.6cm)

Step 2:
Sew the strip set, using the
3/4" Strip Technique where
appropriate (page 18).
Press.

Step 3:
Cut the pieces using either
Method One (page 13) or
Method Two (page 14).

Method One

3" (7.5cm)   2" (5cm)

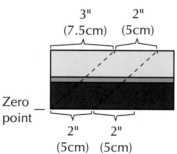

Zero point

2" (5cm)   2" (5cm)

Method Two
45° angle and 1-1/2" (3.6cm) wide

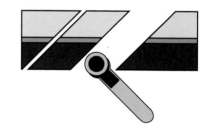

Step 4:
Align the pieces and sew together.
Press without directing the seam
allowances (page 20).

Step 5:
Mark lines for the edging strips
(page 17).

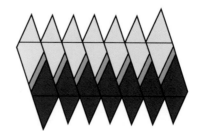

Finished Band Size: 2-1/4" (5.4cm) wide, 18" (43cm) long

Design 39
Angle-Cut, 3/4" Strips

Step 1:
Cut the strips.

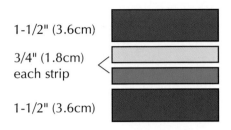

1-1/2" (3.6cm)

3/4" (1.8cm)
each strip

1-1/2" (3.6cm)

Step 2:
Sew the strip set, using the 3/4" Strip Technique where appropriate (page 18). Press.

Step 3:
Cut the pieces using either Method One (page 13) or Method Two (page 14).

Method One

3" (7.5cm)   2" (5cm)

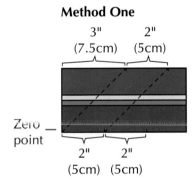

Zero point

2" (5cm)   2" (5cm)

Method Two
45° angle and 1-1/2" (3.6cm) wide

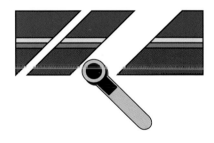

Step 4:
Align the pieces and sew together. Press without directing the seam allowances (page 20).

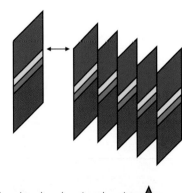

Step 5:
Mark lines for the edging strips (page 17).

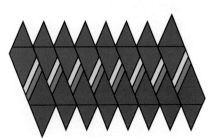

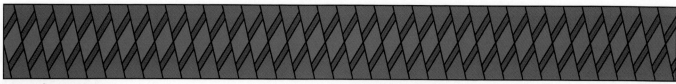

Design 40

Angle-Cut, 3/4" Strips

Finished Band Size: 3-3/4" (9cm) wide, 18" (43cm) long

Step 1:
Cut the strips.

1-1/2" (3.6cm)	
3/4" (1.8cm)	
1-1/4" (3cm)	
3/4" (1.8cm)	
1-1/2" (3.6cm)	

Step 2:
Sew the strip set, using the
3/4" Strip Technique where
appropriate (page 18).
Press.

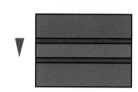

Step 3:
Cut the pieces using either
Method One (page 13) or
Method Two (page 14).

Method One

4"
(10cm) 2"
(5cm)

Zero
point

2"   2"
(5cm) (5cm)

Method Two
45° angle and 1-1/2" (3.6cm) wide

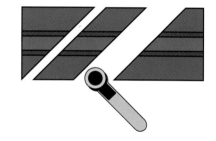

Step 4:
Align the pieces and pin at the
match points on the sewing lines,
rather than on the edges of the
pieces.
Sew together.
Press.

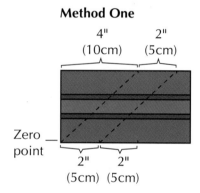

Enlarged view
of alignment

Step 5:
Mark lines for the edging strips
(page 17).

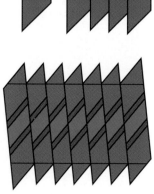

Finished Band Size: 1-1/2" (3.6cm) wide, 30" (72cm) long

Design 41
Angle-Cut, 3/4" Strip, Offset

Step 1:
Cut the strips.

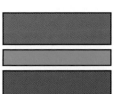

1-1/2" (3.6cm)

3/4" (1.8cm)

1-1/2" (3.6cm)

Step 2:
Sew the strip set, using the 3/4" Strip Technique where appropriate (page 18).
Press.

Step 3:
Mark the strip set with offset line (page 19).

Offset distance 1" (2.4cm)

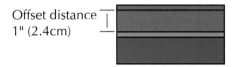

Step 4:
Cut the pieces using either Method One (page 13) or Method Two (page 14).

Method One

1" (2.5cm)   2" (5cm)

Zero point

2" (5cm)   2" (5cm)

Method Two
60° angle and 1-3/4" (4.2cm) wide

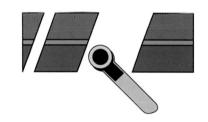

Step 5:
Align the pieces and sew together.
Press.

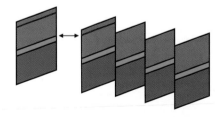

Step 6:
Mark lines for the edging strips (page 17).

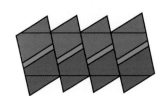

Design 42

Finished Band Size: 2" (5cm) wide, 22" (53cm) long

Angle-Cut, 3/4" Strips, Offset, Multiple Strip Sets

Step 1:
Cut the strips.

a.

1-1/2" (3.6cm)

3/4" (1.8cm)

1-1/2" (3.6cm)

b.

Cut 2 strips:
3/4" (1.8cm)

Step 2:
Sew the a. strip set, using the 3/4" Strip Technique where appropriate (page 18).
Press.

a.

Step 3:
Cut the a. pieces using either Method One (page 13) or Method Two (page 14).

Method One

3" (7.5cm)   2" (5cm)

Zero point

2" (5cm)   2" (5cm)

Method Two
45° angle and 1-1/2" (3.6cm) wide

Step 4:
Cut the b. pieces.
Mark an offset line (page 19) 1/2" (1.2cm) from one end of each b. piece.

b.

3-1/2" (8.4cm)

b.

Offset distance
1/2" (1.2cm)

Step 5:
Align the pieces and sew together, using the 3/4" Strip Technique where appropriate (page 18).
Press.

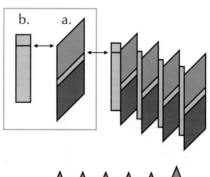

b.   a.

Step 6:
Mark lines for the edging strips (page 17).

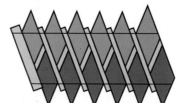

Finished Band Size: 1-1/2" (3.6cm) wide, 36" (86cm) long

Design 43
Straight-Cut Framing, 3/4" Strips

Step 1:
Cut the strips.

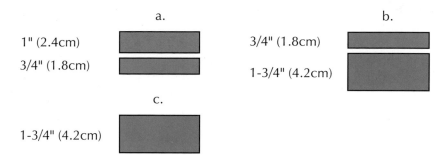

a.

1" (2.4cm)

3/4" (1.8cm)

b.

3/4" (1.8cm)

1-3/4" (4.2cm)

c.

1-3/4" (4.2cm)

Step 2:
Sew the a. and b. strip sets.
Press.

a.

b.

Step 3:
Cut the a. pieces.

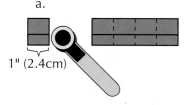

a.

1" (2.4cm)

Step 4:
Sew the a. pieces to the b. strip set, using the 3/4" Strip Technique (page 18). The a. pieces are placed, one at a time, underneath the narrow strip of the b. strip set.
The a. pieces are not sewn to each other but should just touch each other. Do not press.

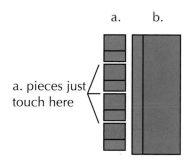

a.   b.

a. pieces just touch here

Step 5:
Sew strip c. to the other side of the a. pieces to make a new d. strip set.
Press.

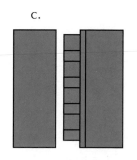

c.

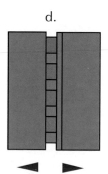

d.

Continued on the next page.

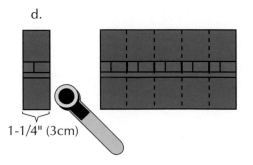

Design 43 continued

Step 6:
Rotate the d. strip set 90°.
Cut the d. strip set (cutting through the holes regardless of the measurement) to make the new d. pieces.

d.

1-1/4" (3cm)

Step 7:
Align the d. pieces and sew together, using the 3/4" Strip Technique (page 18).
Press.

d.

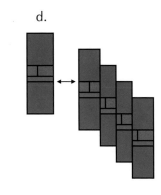

Step 8:
Mark lines for the edging strips (page 17).

Finished Band Size: 1-1/2" (3.6cm) wide, 36" (86cm) long

Design 44
Straight-cut Framing, 3/4" Strips

Follow steps 1–6 in Design 43.

Step 7:
Align the d. pieces and sew together, using the 3/4" Strip Technique (page 18).
Press.

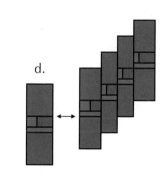

d.

Step 8:
Mark lines for the edging strips (page 17).

Design 45
Straight-cut Framing, 3/4" Strips

Finished Band Size: 1-1/2" (3.6cm) wide, 40" (96cm) long

Step 1:
Cut the strips.

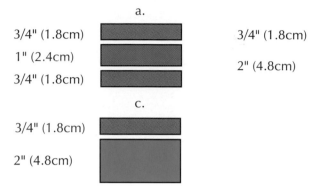

a.
3/4" (1.8cm)
1" (2.4cm)
3/4" (1.8cm)

b.
3/4" (1.8cm)
2" (4.8cm)

c.
3/4" (1.8cm)
2" (4.8cm)

Step 2:
Sew the strip sets.
Press.

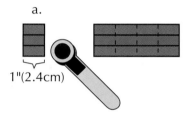

a.   b.   c.

Step 3:
Cut the a. pieces.

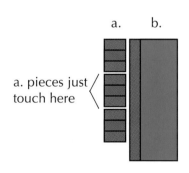

a.
1"(2.4cm)

Step 4:
Sew the a. pieces to the b. strip set, using the 3/4" Strip Technique (page 18). The a. pieces are placed, one at a time, underneath the narrow strip of the b. strip set. The a. pieces are not sewn to each other but should just touch each other.
Do not press.

a.   b.

a. pieces just
touch here

Step 5:
Sew strip set c. to the other side of the a. pieces, using the 3/4" Strip Technique (page 18), to make a new d. strip set.
Press.

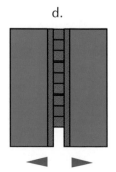

c.   d.

Continued on the next page.

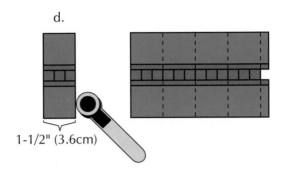

Step 6:
Rotate the d. strip set 90°.
Cut the d. strip set (cutting through the holes regardless of the measurement) to make the new d. pieces.

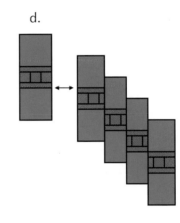

d.

1-1/2" (3.6cm)

Step 7:
Align the d. pieces and sew together, using the 3/4" Strip Technique (page 18).
Press.

d.

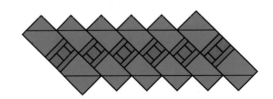

Step 8:
Mark lines for the edging strips (page 17).

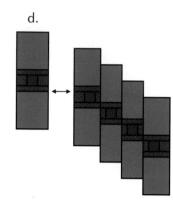

Design 46

Straight-cut Framing, 3/4" Strips

Finished Band Size: 2" (4.8cm) wide, 36" (86cm) long

Follow steps 1–6 in Design 45.

Step 7:
Align the d. pieces and sew together,
using the 3/4" Strip Technique (page 18).
Press.

d.

Step 8:
Mark the lines for the edging strips
(page 17).

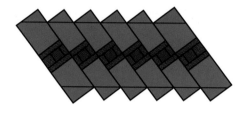

Finished Band Size: 2" (4.8cm) wide, 36" (86cm) long

Step 1:
Cut the strips.

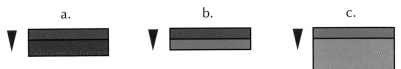

a.
3/4" (1.8cm)
1" (2.4cm)

b.
3/4" (1.8cm)
3/4" (1.8cm)

c.
3/4" (1.8cm)
2" (4.8cm)

d.
2" (4.8cm)

Step 2:
Sew the a., b. and c. strip sets.
Press.

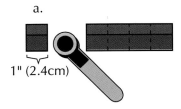

a.   b.   c.

Step 3:
Cut the a. pieces.

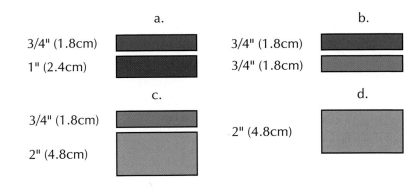

a.

1" (2.4cm)

Step 4:
Sew the a. pieces to the b. strip set,
using the 3/4" Strip Technique (page 18)
to make a new e. strip set. The a. pieces
are placed, one at a time, underneath
the narrow strip of the b. strip set. The
a. pieces are not sewn to each other but
should just touch each other.
Press.

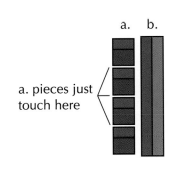

a.   b.

a. pieces just
touch here

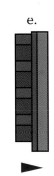

e.

Step 5:
Rotate the e. strip set 90°.
Cut the e. strip set (cutting through
the holes regardless of the
measurement) to make the new
e. pieces.

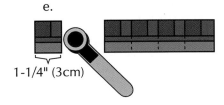

e.

1-1/4" (3cm)

Continued on the next page.

Design 47 continued

Step 6:
Sew the e. pieces to the c. strip set, using the 3/4" Strip Technique (page 18). The e. pieces are placed, one at a time, underneath the narrow strip of the c. strip set.
The e. pieces are not sewn to each other but should just touch each other. Do not press.

c.

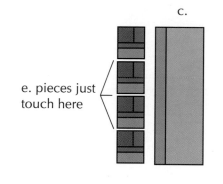

e. pieces just touch here

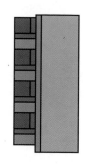

Step 7:
Sew strip d. to the other side of the e. pieces to make a new g. strip set. Press.

d.

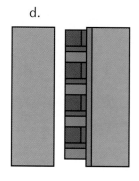

g.

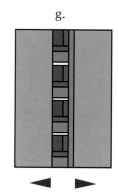

◄ ►

Step 8:
Rotate the g. strip set 90°.
Cut the g. strip set (cutting through the holes regardless of the measurement) to make the new g. pieces.

g.

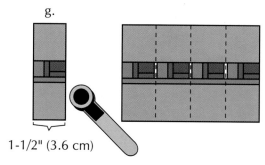

1-1/2" (3.6 cm)

Step 9:
Align the g. pieces and sew together, using the 3/4" Strip Technique (page 18). Press.

g.

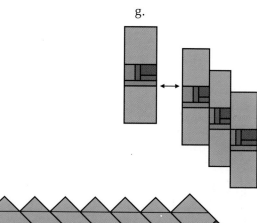

Step 10:
Mark lines for the edging strips (page 17).

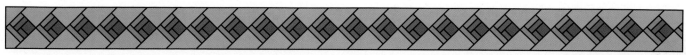

Finished Band Size: 2" (4.8cm) wide, 36" (86cm) long

Design 48
Straight-Cut Framing, 3/4" Strips

Follow steps 1–8 in Design 47.

Step 9:
Align the g. pieces and sew together,
using the 3/4" Strip Technique (page 18).
Press.

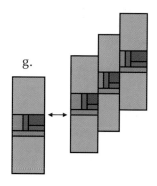

Step 10:
Mark lines for the edging strips
(page 17).

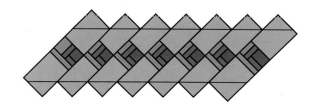

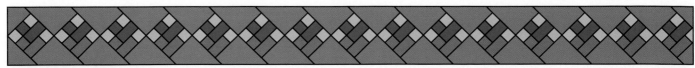

Design 49
Angle-Cut Framing

Finished Band Size: 2-3/4" (6.6cm) wide, 88" (211cm) long

Step 1:
Cut the strips.

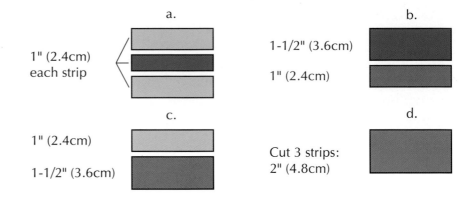

a.

1" (2.4cm)
each strip

b.

1-1/2" (3.6cm)

1" (2.4cm)

c.

1" (2.4cm)

1-1/2" (3.6cm)

d.

Cut 3 strips:
2" (4.8cm)

Step 2:
Sew the a., b. and c. strip sets.
Press.

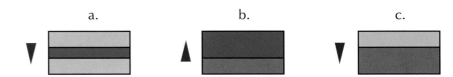

a.   b.   c.

Step 3:
Cut the pieces.

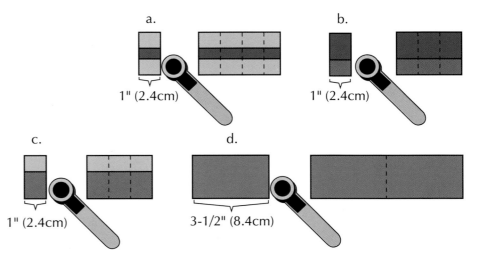

a.

1" (2.4cm)

b.

1" (2.4cm)

c.

1" (2.4cm)

d.

3-1/2" (8.4cm)

Step 4:
Align the a., b. and c. pieces and
sew together to make a new
e. piece.
Some seam allowances will butt.

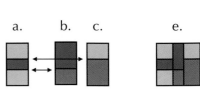

a. b. c.   e.

Continued on the next page.

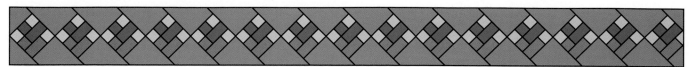

Step 5:
Align the d. and e. pieces and
sew together.
Press.

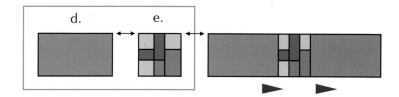

Step 6:
Cut the new f. pieces.
The ends of the angle-cut are 1/2"
from either side of the e. piece.

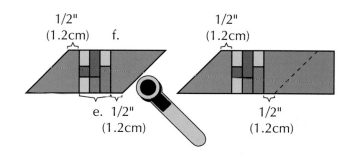

Step 7:
Align the f. pieces and sew together.
Press.

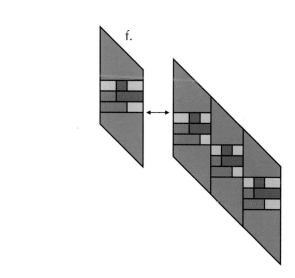

Step 8:
Mark lines for the edging strips
(page 17).

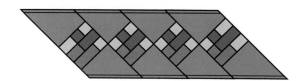

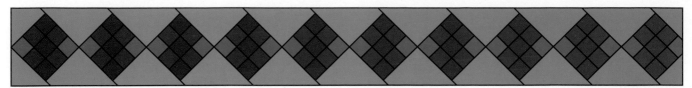

Design 50
Angle-Cut Framing, Upside Down

Finished Band Size: 3-1/2" (8.4cm) wide, 36" (86cm) long

Step 1:
Cut the strips.

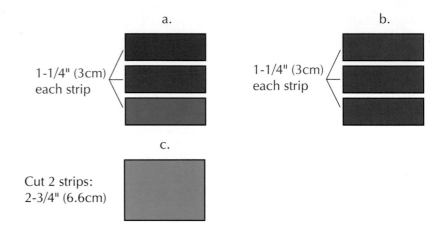

a.

b.

1-1/4" (3cm) each strip

1-1/4" (3cm) each strip

c.

Cut 2 strips: 2-3/4" (6.6cm)

Step 2:
Sew the a. and b. strip sets.
Press.

a.

b.

Step 3:
Cut the a. pieces.
Turn half of the a. pieces upside down to make the d. pieces.
Cut the b. and c. pieces. (Only half of the b. pieces will be used.)

a.

d.

1-1/4" (3cm)

Upside down piece

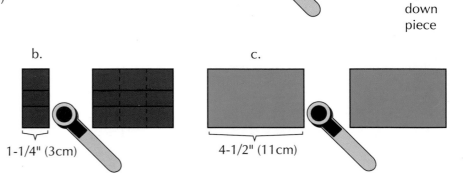

b.

c.

1-1/4" (3cm)

4-1/2" (11cm)

Continued on the next page.

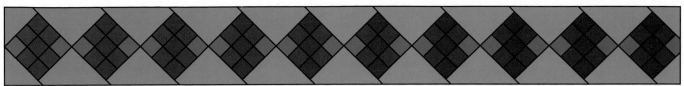

Step 4:
Align the a., b. and d. pieces and sew to make new e. piece. Some seam allowances will butt.

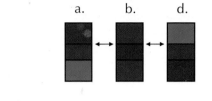

Step 5:
Align the c. and e. pieces and sew together. Press.

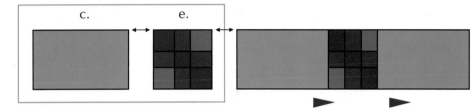

Step 6:
Cut the new f. pieces. The ends of the angle-cut are 1/2" from either side of the e. piece.

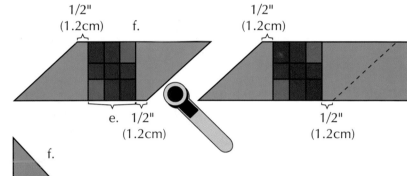

Step 7:
Align the f. pieces and sew together. Press.

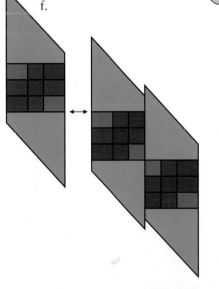

Step 8:
Mark lines for the edging strips (page 17).

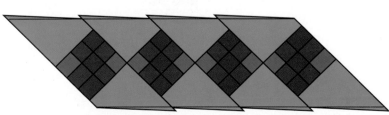

Design 51
Angle-Cut Framing, 3/4" Strips, Upside Down

Finished Band Size: 3-1/4" (7.8cm) wide, 44" (106cm) long

Step 1:
Cut the strips.

a.

1-1/2" (3.6cm)

3/4" (1.8cm)

1-1/2" (3.6cm)

b.

3/4" (1.8cm)

c.

2-3/4" (6.6cm)

Step 2:
Sew the a. strip set, using the 3/4" Strip Technique where appropriate (page 18).
Press.

a.

Step 3:
Cut the a. pieces.
Turn half of the a. pieces upside down to make the d. pieces.
Cut the b. and c. pieces.

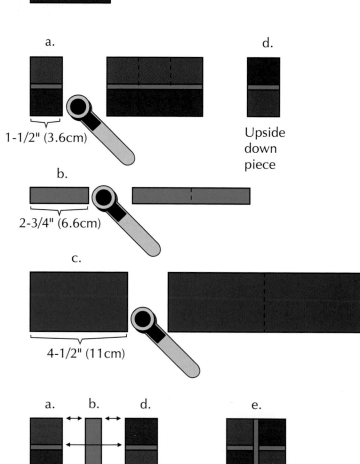

a.

1-1/2" (3.6cm)

d.

Upside down piece

b.

2-3/4" (6.6cm)

c.

4-1/2" (11cm)

Step 4:
Align the a., b. and d. pieces and sew together to make new e. piece, using the 3/4" Strip Technique where appropriate (page 18).

a.   b.   d.   e.

Continued on the next page.

Step 5:
Align the c. and e. pieces
and sew together.
Press.

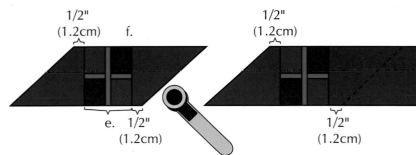

Step 6:
Cut the new f. pieces.
The ends of the angle-cut are 1/2"
from either side of the e. piece.

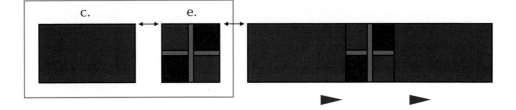

Step 7:
Align the f. pieces and sew
together.
Press.

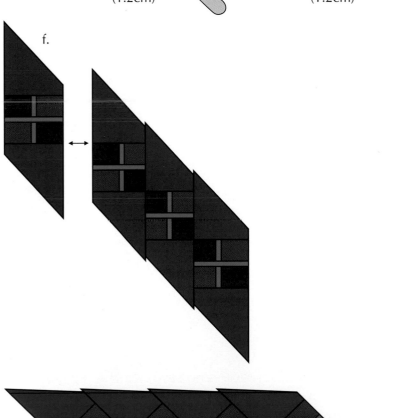

Step 8:
Mark lines for the edging strips
(page 17).

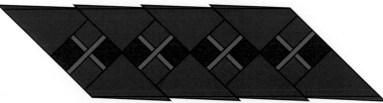

Seminole Design Diagrams   93

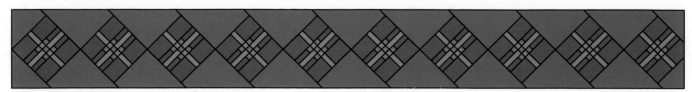

Design 52
Angle-Cut Framing, 3/4" Strips

Finished Band Size: 3-1/2" (8.4cm) wide, 44" (106cm) long

Step 1:
Cut the strips.

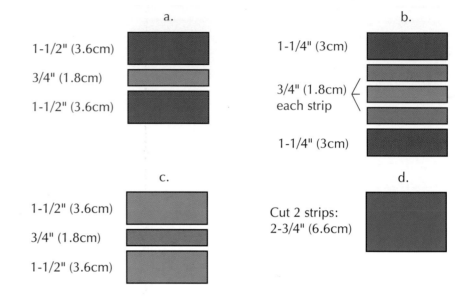

a.
1-1/2" (3.6cm)
3/4" (1.8cm)
1-1/2" (3.6cm)

b.
1-1/4" (3cm)
3/4" (1.8cm)
each strip
1-1/4" (3cm)

c.
1-1/2" (3.6cm)
3/4" (1.8cm)
1-1/2" (3.6cm)

d.
Cut 2 strips:
2-3/4" (6.6cm)

Step 2:
Sew the strip sets, using the 3/4" Strip Technique where appropriate (page 18). Press.

a.   b.   c.

Step 3:
Cut the pieces. (Only half of the c. pieces will be used.)

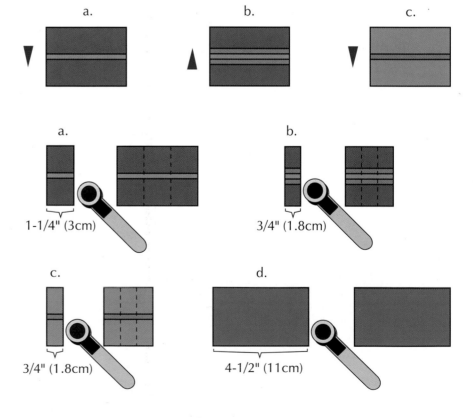

a.
1-1/4" (3cm)

b.
3/4" (1.8cm)

c.
3/4" (1.8cm)

d.
4-1/2" (11cm)

Continued on the next page.

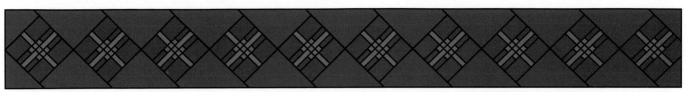

Step 4:

Align a., b. and c. pieces and sew together to make new e. piece, using the 3/4" Strip Technique where appropriate (page 18). Seam allowances will butt.

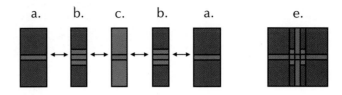

a.   b.   c.   b.   a.   e.

Step 5:

Align the d. and e. pieces and sew together.
Press.

d.   e.

Step 6:

Cut the f. pieces.
The ends of the angle-cut are 1/2" from either side of the e. piece.

1/2" (1.2cm)   f.   1/2" (1.2cm)

e.   1/2" (1.2cm)   1/2" (1.2cm)

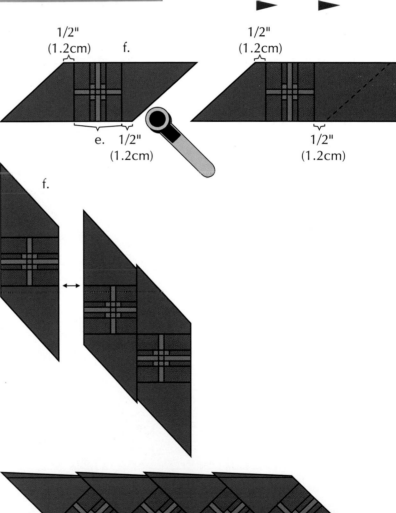

Step 7:

Align the f. pieces and sew together.
Press.

f.

f.

Step 8:

Mark lines for the edging strips (page 17).

Design 53

Finished Band Size: 2" (4.8cm) wide, 16" (38cm) long

Mirror Image, Angle-Cut, Upside Down

Step 1:
Cut the strips.

1-1/2" (3.6cm)
each strip

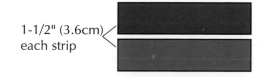

Step 2:
Sew the strip set.
Press.
Fold strip set in half, wrong sides together.

Fold —

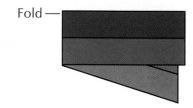

Step 3:
Cut the pieces using either Method One (page 13) or Method Two (page 14).
The pieces from the top will be r. (right-handed) pieces and the pieces from underneath will be l. (left-handed) pieces (page 100).

Method One

2-1/2"   1-3/4"
(6cm)   (4.5cm)

Fold —

Zero
point —

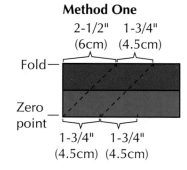

1-3/4"   1-3/4"
(4.5cm)   (4.5cm)

Method Two
45° angle and 1-1/4" (3cm) wide

Fold —

r.   l.

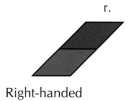

Right-handed   Left-handed

Step 4:
Turn the l. pieces upside down.
Align r. and l. pieces and sew together.
Seam allowances will butt.
Press.

l.

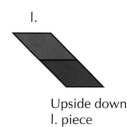

Upside down
l. piece

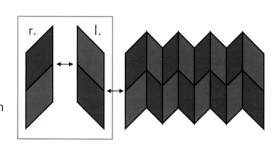

Step 5:
Mark lines for the edging strips (page 17).

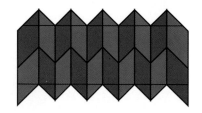

Finished Band Size: 2-1/2" (6cm) wide, 18" (43cm) long

Step 1:
Cut the strips.

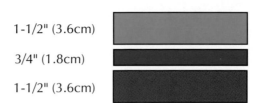

1-1/2" (3.6cm)

3/4" (1.8cm)

1-1/2" (3.6cm)

Step 2:
Sew the strip set, using the 3/4"
Strip Technique (page 18).
Press.
Fold strip set in half, wrong
sides together.

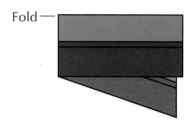

Fold

Step 3:
Cut the pieces using either
Method One (page 13) or
Method Two (page 14).
The pieces from the top will
be r. (right-handed) pieces
and the pieces from
underneath will be l. (left-
handed) pieces (page 100).

Method One

3"   2"
(7.5cm)   (5cm)

Fold

Zero
point

2"   2"
(5cm)   (5cm)

Method Two
45° angle and 1-1/2" (3.6cm) wide

Fold

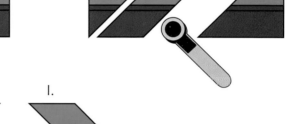

r.   l.

Right-handed   Left-handed

Step 4:
Align r. and l. pieces and sew
together.
Press.

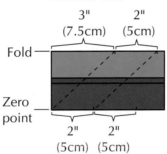

Step 5:
Mark lines for the edging strips
(page 17).

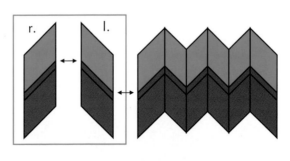

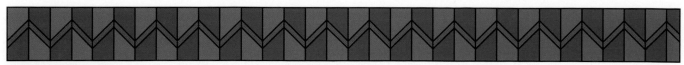

Design 55

Finished Band Size: 2-1/2" (6cm) wide, 18" (43cm) long

Mirror Image, Angle-Cut, 3/4" Strip, Upside Down

Follow steps 1–3 in Design 54.

Step 4:
Turn the l. pieces upside down.
Align r. and l. pieces and sew together.
Seam allowances will butt.
Press.

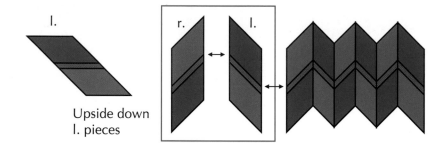

Upside down
l. pieces

Step 5:
Mark lines for the edging strips (page 17).

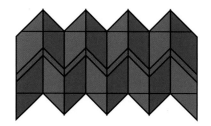

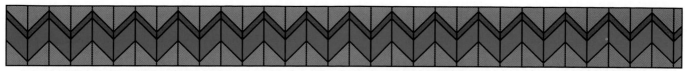

Finished Band Size: 2-3/4" (6.6cm) wide, 18" (43cm) long

Design 56
Mirror Image, Angle-Cut, 3/4" Strip

Step 1:
Cut the strips.

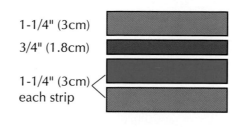

1-1/4" (3cm)

3/4" (1.8cm)

1-1/4" (3cm)
each strip

Step 2:
Sew the strip set, using the 3/4" Strip Technique where appropriate (page 18).
Press.
Fold strip set in half, wrong sides together.

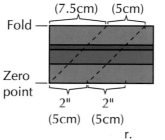

Fold

Step 3:
Cut the pieces using either Method One (page 13) or Method Two (page 14).
The pieces from the top will be r. (right handed) pieces and the pieces from underneath will be l. (left handed) pieces (page 100).

Method One

3" (7.5cm)   2" (5cm)

Fold

Zero point

2" (5cm)   2" (5cm)

r.

Right-handed

Method Two
45° angle and 1-1/2" (3.6cm) wide

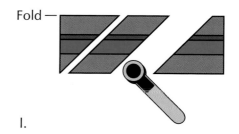

Fold

l.

Left-handed

Step 4:
Align r. and l. pieces and sew together.
Press.

r.   l.

Step 5:
Mark lines for the edging strips (page 17).

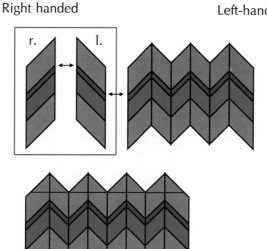

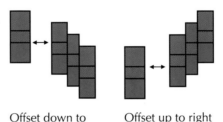

6. Additional Seminole Patchwork Construction

Construction of Mirror Image Designs

There are several uses of mirror image in Seminole patchwork. Chevron designs (Designs 53 through 56) are created when mirror image pieces are cut and alternated in a patchwork band. Mirror image patchwork bands are used in the design of symmetrical quilt borders and in garments, such as shirt yokes. Further design variations are possible by sewing mirror image bands to each other lengthwise. Since all designs are not appropriate for mirror image effects, you will want to experiment by holding the edge of a mirror against the design diagrams. Some very successful mirror image designs are shown in this section.

To sew identical strip sets for these effects, it is important to sew each strip set in the same order as the others. If strip *a* is first sewn to strip *b* and strip *c* is added last, sew all of the strip sets in this same order.

Mirror Image Bands from Straight-Cut Pieces

To make mirror image bands from straight-cut pieces, all the pieces are cut the same and the mirror image is achieved when the pieces are offset and sewn together. For one band, the pieces are offset *down* to the right. For the second band, the pieces are offset *up* to the right. Complete one band before beginning to sew the mirror image band.

Reversing the offset will result in two bands that appear to be reflections of each other.

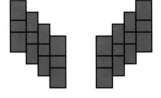

Offset down to right   Offset up to right

Aligning straight-cut pieces to sew mirror image bands

Mirror image bands from straight-cut pieces

Mirror Image Bands from Angle-Cut Pieces

Identical strip sets, wrong sides together

Right-handed piece

Left-handed pieces (wrong side and face side)

Cutting angle-cut pieces for mirror image effects

To make mirror image bands from angle-cut pieces, mirror image pieces must be cut. Sew and press two identical strip sets and place them wrong sides together. Use a ruler as described in Methods One or Two of Chapter 3 to mark the pieces, and cut through both layers. If a rotary cutter is used, take extra care to hold the ruler in position and use extra pressure on the blade as it slices through the stacked seam allowances. If cutting with scissors, place a few pins through both layers of each marked piece to keep the layers from shifting. The pieces cut from the top strip set will be face side up and are called right-handed pieces. The pieces cut from the bottom strip set will be wrong side up. They are mirror images of the right-handed pieces and are called left-handed pieces.

To sew all the right-handed pieces together into a right-handed band of patchwork, follow the diagram for that design. This example uses pieces from Design 38 to show the right-handed pieces with the match points, the beige corner and aqua point, aligned. The pieces are placed face sides together with the piece to the right on top, the beige corner placed on the aqua point, and sewn.

As the mirror image angle-cut pieces are cut and collected, keep them in separate stacks, with the right-handed pieces face side up and the left-handed pieces wrong side up.

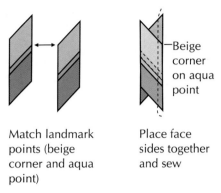

Match landmark points (beige corner and aqua point)

Place face sides together and sew

—Beige corner on aqua point

Align and sew right-handed pieces

To sew the left-handed pieces together, align the same match points. This time when the pieces are placed face sides together with the piece to the right on top, the aqua point is placed on the beige corner. The same match points are being used, but the opposite one is on top.

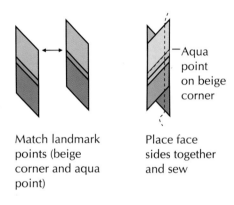

Match landmark points (beige corner and aqua point)

Place face sides together and sew

—Aqua point on beige corner

Align and sew left-handed pieces

To avoid confusion, sew all of the right-handed pieces together into a right-handed band of patchwork before sewing the left-handed pieces together.

Here are mirror image bands of Design 38, with edging strips in place and ready to use as shirt yokes.

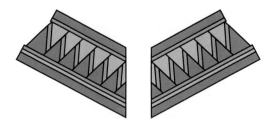

Mirror image shirt yokes

Straight-Cut Pieces
Turning Corners

Mirror image bands of straight-cut pieces turn neatly to make two of the four corners of a frame or other four-sided figure. Special pieces will have to be sewn for the other two corners.

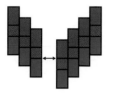 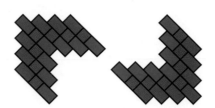 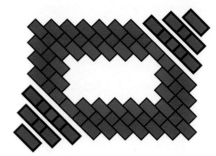

 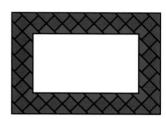

a. Sew mirror image bands

b. One corner sewn

c. Two diagonally opposite corners

d. Frame assembly with two mirror image corners and special pieces for other corners (heavy outline)

e. Frame sewn

f. Frame finished

Assembling a frame with straight-cut pieces

Angle-Cut Pieces
Turning Corners

Mirror image bands of angle-cut pieces can turn all four corners on a frame. Use two bands sewn with right-handed pieces and two sewn with left-handed pieces.

Trim each band before sewing them together. Align the ruler cutting guide with the line of the innermost raw edges of the band and the outer design points, as shown for marking edging strips. Cut off the jagged edges of the bands along the edge of the ruler cutting guide. These newly cut edges of the band become guidelines for cutting the ends of the band at the 45° angle necessary for frame corners. Allow 1/4" (0.6cm) seam allowances when cutting the ends. Pin the ends of the bands to match the design points before sewing together. If edging strips are used, sew them on the patchwork bands before making 45° angle cuts on the ends of the bands.

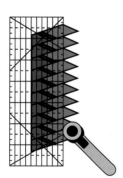 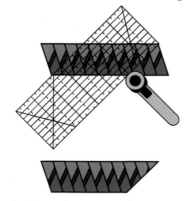  

a. Trim edges of band

b. Cut ends at 45° angles

c. Frame assembly

d. Frame finished

Assembling a frame with angle-cut pieces

Mirror image bands can be sewn together at any angle for special effects, such as V-necks on garments. The effect is different depending on which ends are sewn together.

Joining different ends produces different effects

Wonderful designs emerge when mirror image bands are sewn together lengthwise. Trim the jagged edges off the bands and pin the design points together along the 1/4" (0.6cm) seam line. Sew the bands together with the seam allowances pointing toward you, if possible, to keep the seam line tidy. Notice that different effects result from changes in the position of the trimming line, showing more or less of the inside fabric color.

Design 38 in mirror image with different effects created when the position of the trimming line is changed

The combined bands will look different with the colors reversed.

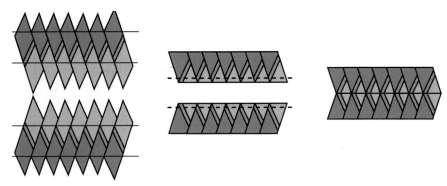

Design 38 in mirror image with colors reversed

Two more designs made with mirror image bands are shown below.

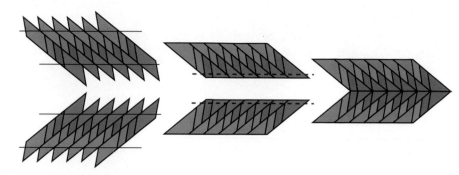

Design 36 in mirror image

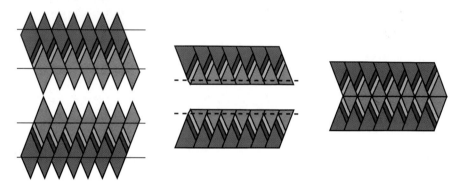

Design 39 in mirror image

Construction of Graphed Designs

Delightful pictorial designs planned on 1/4" graph paper and constructed using Seminole patchwork techniques are easier and faster to sew than their complicated appearances suggest. The simplest designs are symmetrical (the same shape on both sides) and involve only a few pieces (vertical columns) to make one design. Success with graphed designs requires accurate seam allowances and use of the 3/4" Strip Technique every time a 3/4" (1.8cm) strip or piece is sewn. If the scale is changed to larger squares, the 3/4" Strip Technique does not apply.

A Graphed Design Exercise

#1 #2 #3 #4 #5

The heart exercise

A very simple graphed design is a heart in three colors. The following steps show how to plan and sew this design.

Step 1. Draw the design with colored pencils on 1/4" graph paper. Allow for at least 1/2" (1.2cm) of background above and below the pictorial design, plus 1/4" (0.6cm) for edging strip seam allowances at the top and bottom.

Step 2. Redraw the design as separate 1/4" (0.6cm) wide vertical columns. Each column will be a piece in the Seminole construction. Notice that columns #1 and #5 are identical and columns #2 and #4 are identical.

Step 3. Plan the strip sets from which the pieces will be cut. Since columns #1 and #5 are identical, only one strip set will be sewn for both of those columns. For the same reason, only one strip set will be sewn for columns #2 and #4. This is why symmetrical designs are easier to make. Next to each color in each vertical column, write the width of that color plus two 1/4" (0.6cm) seam allowances. This will be the width to cut the strips for each strip set.

Step 4. Cut the strips and sew the strip set for each vertical column. Use the 3/4" Strip Technique whenever appropriate. Graphed designs are often used for small projects., so full length strips may be longer than needed. Cut the strips in half or 20" (50cm) long. Several strips of the same width and color are often needed for the multiple strip sets. Six or seven individual designs can be sewn from strip sets 20" (50cm) long.

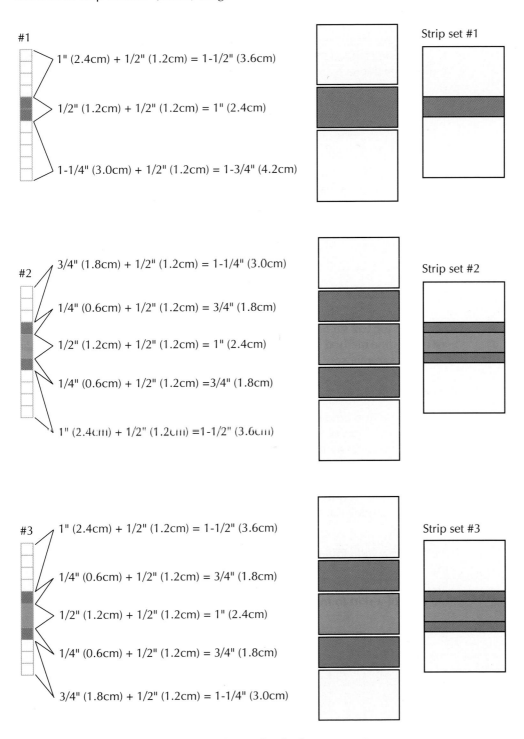

#1

1" (2.4cm) + 1/2" (1.2cm) = 1-1/2" (3.6cm)

1/2" (1.2cm) + 1/2" (1.2cm) = 1" (2.4cm)

1-1/4" (3.0cm) + 1/2" (1.2cm) = 1-3/4" (4.2cm)

Strip set #1

#2

3/4" (1.8cm) + 1/2" (1.2cm) = 1-1/4" (3.0cm)

1/4" (0.6cm) + 1/2" (1.2cm) = 3/4" (1.8cm)

1/2" (1.2cm) + 1/2" (1.2cm) = 1" (2.4cm)

1/4" (0.6cm) + 1/2" (1.2cm) =3/4" (1.8cm)

1" (2.4cm) + 1/2" (1.2cm) =1-1/2" (3.6cm)

Strip set #2

#3

1" (2.4cm) + 1/2" (1.2cm) = 1-1/2" (3.6cm)

1/4" (0.6cm) + 1/2" (1.2cm) = 3/4" (1.8cm)

1/2" (1.2cm) + 1/2" (1.2cm) = 1" (2.4cm)

1/4" (0.6cm) + 1/2" (1.2cm) = 3/4" (1.8cm)

3/4" (1.8cm) + 1/2" (1.2cm) = 1-1/4" (3.0cm)

Strip set #3

The three strip sets for the heart exercise

Step 5. Press the strip sets carefully to be sure the finished width of each strip matches the width in the drawing.

Step 6. Cut two pieces each from the middle of strip sets #1 (to create pieces #1 and #5) and #2 (to create pieces #2 and #4) and one piece from the middle of strip set #3 (to create piece #3). Cut each piece 3/4" (1.8cm) wide. These are test pieces to assure that the design will fit together. If the pieces do not match, adjustments can be made before all the pieces are cut.

Step 7. Sew the pieces together from right to left (from piece #5 to piece #1) to make one graphed design, using the 3/4" Strip Technique so that the finished width of each piece is exactly 1/4" (0.6cm). Use pins to match the seam lines on the pieces.

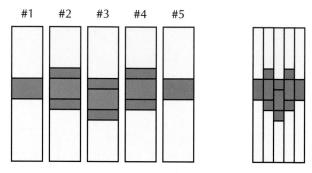

Sewing the strip sets from right to left beginning with piece #5

Step 8. If the test section fits together, cut and sew the rest of the pieces. An assembly line method is the most efficient way to sew many designs together. For this example, sew all the #5 pieces to all the #4 pieces. Then, using the 3/4" Strip Technique, add all the #3 pieces, then all the #2 pieces, and finally sew on all the #1 pieces.

If the test section *does not* fit together, first try creative pressing with the point of the iron and lots of steam to narrow or widen the errant strips. If that does not help, resew to narrow or widen the seam allowances on those strips. It is a consolation that these alterations can all be done at once on the strip set, instead of having to alter each piece. Consider the intended use of the designs when deciding how much time to spend perfectly matching each seam. A few designs on a book cover will get closer scrutiny than many designs bordering a skirt.

Step 9. Sew individual designs directly to each other or to spacer pieces cut from the background fabric. Designs could be spaced close together on small items, such as the yoke of a toddler's overalls, but could be widely spaced on the hem of a skirt to make a few designs go a long way.

Spacer pieces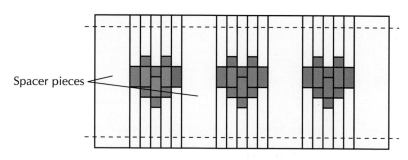

Sewing the designs to spacer pieces

Ideas for graphed designs can come from needlework books, and it is easy to create designs by doodling with graph paper and colored pencils. The following design ideas include some variations in spacing.

Graphed Designs

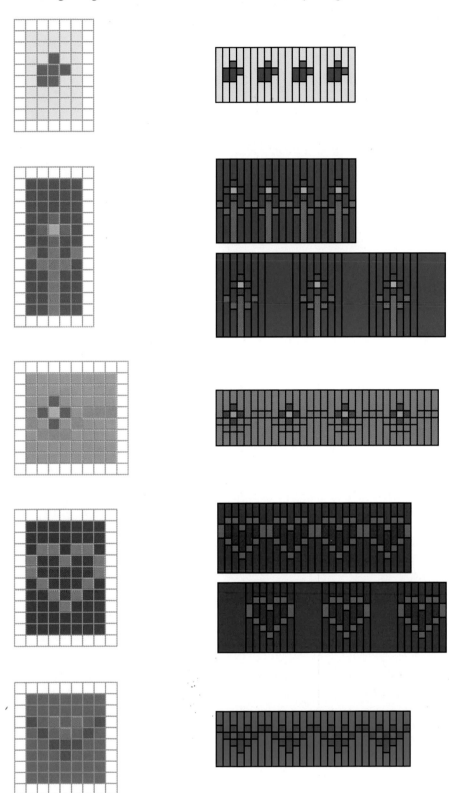

Additional graphed designs

Bibliography

Seminole Patchwork

Allison, Linda, and Allison, Stella. *Rags: Making a Little Something Out of Almost Nothing.* New York: Clarkson N. Potter, 1979.

Bradkin, Cheryl Greider. *The Seminole Patchwork Book.* Carmichael, CA: Bradkin, Cheryl, 1978.

———. *The Seminole Patchwork Book.* Atlanta, GA: Yours Truly, 1980.

Brandebourg, Margaret. *Seminole Patchwork.* London: B T Batsford, 1987.

Campbell-Harding, Valerie. *Strip Patchwork.* New York: Dover Publications, 1983.

Denton, Susan and Macey, Barbara. *Quiltmaking.* New York: Sterling Publishing Co., 1988.

Dudley, Taimi. *Strip Patchwork.* New York: Van Nostrand Reinhold, 1980.

French Chic Quilting Patchwork and Applique. New York: Ballantine Books, 1986.

Garbarino, Merwyn S. *The Seminole.* New York: Chelsea House Publishers, 1989.

James, Michael. The *Quiltmaker's Handbook.* Englewood Cliffs, NJ: Prentice-Hall, 1978.

Lambert, Nancy Devlin. *Guide to Seminole Patchwork.* Severna Park, MD: Starshine Stitchery Press, 1983.

Meilach, Dona Z. and Menagh, Dee. *Exotic Needlework.* New York: Crown Publishers, 1978.

Onoyama, Takae. *Seminole Patchwork.* Japan: Shufunotomo Co., 1983.

Rush, Beverly and Wittman, Lassie. *The Complete Book of Seminole Patchwork.* Seattle, WA: Madrona Publishers, 1982.

The Seminole Research Design Project. *Seminole Patchwork Principles and Designs.* New York: The Seminole Research Design Project, 1980.

Seward, Linda. *The Complete Book of Patchwork, Quilting and Applique.* New York: Prentice-Hall Press, 1987.

Wood, Margaret. *Native American Fashion: Modern Adaptations of Traditional Designs.* New York: Van Nostrand Reinhold, 1981.

Wittman, Lassie. *Seminole Patchwork Patterns.* Bellevue WA: Wittman, Lassie, 1979.

Machine Quilting

Fanning, Robbie and Fanning, Tony. *The Complete Book of Machine Quilting.* Radnor, PA: Chilton Book Company, 1980.

Hargrave, Harriet. *Heirloom Machine Quilting.* Lafayette, CA: C & T Publishing, 1990.

Clothing

Leone, Diana. In*vestments.* Mountain View, CA: Leone Publications, 1982.

Cheryl Greider Bradkin grew up in the San Francisco Bay Area and had an early introduction to the textiles of many cultures through her mother's collection of ethnic clothing. Cheryl received a degree in zoology from the University of California at Berkeley and worked as a biologist, with crafts always in progress. She began sewing Seminole patchwork in 1977 and found the technique successfully combined the precision of her scientific education with her love of color and fabric. She has taught workshops on Seminole patchwork in the U.S., Canada and Japan. Her community interests include serving on the advisory boards for a textile library and for the park district. She lives in Sacramento, California with her husband, Bill, and their daughter, Lisa.

Books from Leone Publications

The Sampler Quilt, Diana Leone..$11.95

Fine Hand Quilting, Diana Leone... $12.95

Quiltmaker's Book of 6" Patterns, Anthony & Lehman......................$12.95

Attic Windows, Diana Leone.. $14.95

Investments, Diana Leone.. $14.95

Sampler Supreme, Catherine Anthony..$14.95

Quiltmaker's Big Book of Grids, Anthony & Lehman........................$14.95

Morning Star Quilts, Florence Pulford   Soft cover.......................... $24.95
Hard cover,
                    collector's edition............$34.95

To order books:

Leone Publications, Dept SP
2628 Bayshore Parkway
Mountain View, CA 94043

(415) 965-9797

For more information, send a self-addressed, stamped, legal size envelope.